Timaeus

Plato

Translated with an introduction by Benjamin Jowett

ISBN-13: 978-1724243485

ISBN-10: 1724243489

Introduction and Analysis.

Of all the writings of Plato the Timaeus is the most obscure and repulsive to the modern reader, and has nevertheless had the greatest influence over the ancient and mediaeval world. The obscurity arises in the infancy of physical science, out of the confusion of theological, mathematical, and physiological notions, out of the desire to conceive the whole of nature without any adequate knowledge of the parts, and from a greater perception of similarities which lie on the surface than of differences which are hidden from view. To bring sense under the control of reason; to find some way through the mist or labyrinth of appearances, either the highway of mathematics, or more devious paths suggested by the analogy of man with the world, and of the world with man; to see that all things have a cause and are tending towards an end — this is the spirit of the ancient physical philosopher. He has no notion of trying an experiment and is hardly capable of observing the curiosities of nature which are 'tumbling out at his feet,' or of interpreting even the most obvious of them. He is driven back from the nearer to the more distant, from particulars to generalities, from the earth to the stars. He lifts up his eyes to the heavens and seeks to guide by their motions his erring footsteps. But we neither appreciate the conditions of knowledge to which he was subjected, nor have the ideas which fastened upon his imagination the same hold upon us. For he is hanging between matter and mind; he is under the dominion at the same time both of sense and of abstractions; his impressions are taken almost at random from the outside of nature; he sees the light, but not the objects which are revealed by the light; and he brings into juxtaposition things which to us appear wide as the poles asunder, because he finds nothing between them. He passes abruptly from persons to ideas and numbers, and from ideas and numbers to persons — from the heavens to man, from astronomy to physiology; he confuses, or rather does not distinguish, subject and object, first and final causes, and is dreaming of geometrical figures lost in a flux of sense. He contrasts the perfect movements of the heavenly bodies with the imperfect representation of them (Rep.), and he does not always require strict accuracy even in applications of number and figure (Rep.). His mind lingers around the forms of mythology, which he uses as symbols or translates into figures of speech. He has no implements of observation, such as the telescope or microscope; the great science of chemistry is a blank to him. It is only by an effort that the modern thinker can breathe the atmosphere of the ancient philosopher, or understand how, under such unequal conditions, he seems in many instances, by a sort of inspiration, to have anticipated the truth.

The influence with the Timaeus has exercised upon posterity is due partly to a misunderstanding. In the supposed depths of this dialogue the Neo-Platonists found hidden meanings and connections with the Jewish and Christian Scriptures, and out of them they elicited doctrines quite at variance with the spirit of Plato. Believing that he was inspired by the Holy Ghost, or had received his wisdom from Moses, they seemed to find in his writings the Christian Trinity, the Word, the Church, the creation of the world in a Jewish sense, as they really found the personality of God or of mind, and the immortality of the soul. All religions and philosophies met and mingled in the schools of Alexandria, and the Neo-Platonists had a method of interpretation which could elicit any meaning out of any words. They were really incapable of distinguishing between the opinions of one philosopher and another — between Aristotle and Plato, or between the serious thoughts of Plato and his passing fancies. They were absorbed in his theology and were under the dominion of his name, while that which was truly great and truly characteristic in him, his effort to realize and connect abstractions, was not understood by them at all. Yet the genius of Plato and Greek philosophy reacted upon the East, and a Greek element of thought and language overlaid and partly reduced to order the chaos of Orientalism. And kindred spirits, like St. Augustine, even though they were acquainted with his writings only through the medium of a Latin translation, were profoundly affected by them, seeming to find 'God and his word everywhere insinuated' in them (August. Confess.)

There is no danger of the modern commentators on the Timaeus falling into the absurdities of the Neo-Platonists. In the present day we are well aware that an ancient philosopher is to be interpreted from himself and by the contemporary history of thought. We know that mysticism is not criticism. The fancies of the Neo-Platonists are only interesting to us because they exhibit a phase of the human mind which prevailed widely in the first centuries of the Christian era, and is not wholly extinct in our own day. But they have nothing to do with the interpretation of Plato, and in spirit they are opposed to him. They are the feeble expression of an age which has lost the power not only of creating great works, but of understanding them. They are the spurious birth of a marriage between philosophy and tradition, between Hellas and the East —(Greek) (Rep.). Whereas the so-called mysticism of Plato is purely Greek, arising out of his imperfect knowledge and high aspirations, and is the growth of an age in which philosophy is not wholly separated from poetry and mythology.

A greater danger with modern interpreters of Plato is the tendency to regard the Timaeus as the centre of his system. We do not know how Plato would have arranged his own dialogues, or whether the thought of arranging any of them, besides the two 'Trilogies' which he has expressly connected; was ever present to his mind. But, if he had arranged them, there are many indications that this is not the place which he would have assigned to the Timaeus. We observe, first of all, that the dialogue is put into the mouth of a Pythagorean philosopher, and not of Socrates. And this is required by dramatic propriety; for the investigation of nature was expressly renounced by Socrates in the Phaedo. Nor does Plato himself attribute any importance to his guesses at science. He is not at all absorbed by them, as he is by the IDEA of good. He is modest and hesitating, and confesses that his words partake of the uncertainty of the subject (Tim.). The dialogue is primarily concerned with the animal creation, including under this term the heavenly bodies, and with man only as one among the animals. But we can hardly suppose that Plato would have preferred the study of nature to man, or that he would have deemed the formation of the world and the human frame to have the same interest which he ascribes to the mystery of being and not-being, or to the great political problems which he discusses in the Republic and the Laws. There are no speculations on physics in the other dialogues of Plato, and he himself regards the consideration of them as a rational pastime only. He is beginning to feel the need of further divisions of knowledge; and is becoming aware that besides dialectic, mathematics, and the arts, there is another field which has been hitherto unexplored by him. But he has not as yet defined this intermediate territory which lies somewhere between medicine and mathematics, and he would have felt that there was as great an impiety in ranking theories of physics first in the order of knowledge, as in placing the body before the soul.

It is true, however, that the Timaeus is by no means confined to speculations on physics. The deeper foundations of the Platonic philosophy, such as the nature of God, the distinction of the sensible and intellectual, the great original conceptions of time and space, also appear in it. They are found principally in the first half of the dialogue. The construction of the heavens is for the most part ideal; the cyclic year serves as the connection between the world of absolute being and of generation, just as the number of population in the Republic is the expression or symbol of the transition from the ideal to the actual state. In some passages we are uncertain whether we are reading a description of astronomical facts or contemplating processes of the human mind, or of that divine mind (Phil.) which in Plato is hardly separable from it. The characteristics of man are transferred to the world-animal, as for example when intelligence and knowledge are said to be perfected by the circle of the Same, and true opinion by the circle of the Other; and conversely the motions of the world-animal reappear in man; its amorphous state continues in the child, and in both disorder and chaos are gradually succeeded by stability and order. It is not however to passages like these that Plato is referring when he speaks of the uncertainty of his subject, but rather to the composition of bodies, to the relations of colours, the nature of diseases, and the like, about which he truly feels the lamentable ignorance prevailing in his own age.

We are led by Plato himself to regard the Timaeus, not as the centre or inmost shrine of the edifice, but as a detached building in a different style, framed, not after the Socratic, but after some Pythagorean model. As in the Cratylus and Parmenides, we are uncertain whether Plato is expressing his own opinions, or appropriating and perhaps improving the philosophical speculations of others. In all three dialogues he is exerting his dramatic and imitative power; in the Cratylus mingling a satirical and humorous purpose with true principles of language; in the Parmenides overthrowing Megarianism by a sort of ultra-Megarianism, which discovers contradictions in the one as great as those which have been previously shown to exist in the ideas. There is a similar uncertainty about the Timaeus; in the first part he scales the heights of transcendentalism, in the latter part he treats in a bald and superficial manner of the functions and diseases of the human frame. He uses the thoughts and almost the words of Parmenides when he discourses of being and of essence, adopting from old religion into philosophy the conception of God, and from the Megarians the IDEA of good. He agrees with Empedocles and the Atomists in attributing the greater differences of kinds to the figures of the elements and their movements into and out of one another. With Heracleitus, he acknowledges the perpetual flux; like Anaxagoras, he asserts the predominance of mind, although admitting an element of necessity which reason is incapable of subduing; like the Pythagoreans he supposes the mystery of the world to be contained in number. Many, if not all the elements of the Pre-Socratic philosophy are included in the Timaeus. It is a composite or eclectic work of imagination, in which Plato, without naming them, gathers up into a kind of system the various elements of philosophy which preceded him.

If we allow for the difference of subject, and for some growth in Plato's own mind, the discrepancy between the Timaeus and the other dialogues will not appear to be great. It is probable that the relation of the ideas to God or of God to the world was differently conceived by him at different times of his life. In all his later dialogues we observe a tendency in him to personify mind or God, and he therefore naturally inclines to view creation as the work of design. The creator is like a human artist who frames in his mind a plan which he executes by the help of his servants. Thus the language of philosophy which speaks of first and second causes is crossed by another sort of phraseology: 'God made the world because he was good, and the demons ministered to him.' The Timaeus is cast in a more theological and less philosophical mould than the other dialogues, but the same general spirit is apparent; there is the same dualism or opposition between the ideal and actual — the soul is prior to the body, the intelligible and unseen to the visible and corporeal. There is the same distinction between knowledge and opinion which occurs in the Theaetetus and Republic, the same enmity to the poets, the same combination of music and gymnastics. The doctrine of transmigration is still held by him, as in the Phaedrus and Republic; and the soul has a view of the heavens in a prior state of being. The ideas also remain, but they have become types in nature, forms of men, animals, birds, fishes. And the attribution of evil to physical causes accords with the doctrine which he maintains in the Laws respecting the involuntariness of vice.

The style and plan of the Timaeus differ greatly from that of any other of the Platonic dialogues. The language is weighty, abrupt, and in some passages sublime. But Plato has not the same mastery over his instrument which he exhibits in the Phaedrus or Symposium. Nothing can exceed the beauty or art of the introduction, in which he is using words after his accustomed manner. But in the rest of the work the power of language seems to fail him, and the dramatic form is wholly given up. He could write in one style, but not in another, and the Greek language had not as yet been fashioned by any poet or philosopher to describe physical phenomena. The early physiologists had generally written in verse; the prose writers, like Democritus and Anaxagoras, as far as we can judge from their fragments, never attained to a periodic style. And hence we find the same sort of clumsiness in the Timaeus of Plato which characterizes the philosophical poem of Lucretius. There is a want of flow and often a defect of rhythm; the meaning is sometimes obscure, and there is a greater use of apposition and more of repetition than occurs in Plato's earlier writings. The sentences are less closely connected and also more involved; the antecedents of demonstrative and relative pronouns are in some cases remote and perplexing. The greater frequency of participles and of absolute constructions gives the effect of heaviness. The descriptive portion of the Timaeus retains traces of the first Greek prose composition; for the great master of language was speaking on a theme with which he was imperfectly acquainted, and had no words in which to express his meaning.

The rugged grandeur of the opening discourse of Timaeus may be compared with the more harmonious beauty of a similar passage in the Phaedrus.

To the same cause we may attribute the want of plan. Plato had not the command of his materials which would have enabled him to produce a perfect work of art. Hence there are several new beginnings and resumptions and formal or artificial connections; we miss the 'callida junctura' of the earlier dialogues. His speculations about the Eternal, his theories of creation, his mathematical anticipations, are supplemented by desultory remarks on the one immortal and the two mortal souls of man, on the functions of the bodily organs in health and disease, on sight, hearing, smell, taste, and touch. He soars into the heavens, and then, as if his wings were suddenly clipped, he walks ungracefully and with difficulty upon the earth. The greatest things in the world, and the least things in man, are brought within the compass of a short treatise. But the intermediate links are missing, and we cannot be surprised that there should be a want of unity in a work which embraces astronomy, theology, physiology, and natural philosophy in a few pages.

It is not easy to determine how Plato's cosmos may be presented to the reader in a clearer and shorter form; or how we may supply a thread of connexion to his ideas without giving greater consistency to them than they possessed in his mind, or adding on consequences which would never have occurred to him. For he has glimpses of the truth, but no comprehensive or perfect vision. There are isolated expressions about the nature of God which have a wonderful depth and power; but we are not justified in assuming that these had any greater significance to the mind of Plato than language of a neutral and impersonal character . . . With a view to the illustration of the Timaeus I propose to divide this Introduction into sections, of which the first will contain an outline of the dialogue: (2) I shall consider the aspects of nature which presented themselves to Plato and his age, and the elements of philosophy which entered into the conception of them: (3) the theology and physics of the Timaeus, including the soul of the world, the conception of time and space, and the composition of the elements: (4) in the fourth section I shall consider the Platonic astronomy, and the position of the earth. There will remain, (5) the psychology, (6) the physiology of Plato, and (7) his analysis of the senses to be briefly commented upon: (8) lastly, we may examine in what points Plato approaches or anticipates the discoveries of modern science.

Section 1.

Socrates begins the Timaeus with a summary of the Republic. He lightly touches upon a few points — the division of labour and distribution of the citizens into classes, the double nature and training of the guardians, the community of property and of women and children. But he makes no mention of the second education, or of the government of philosophers.

And now he desires to see the ideal State set in motion; he would like to know how she behaved in some great struggle. But he is unable to invent such a narrative himself; and he is afraid that the poets are equally incapable; for, although he pretends to have nothing to say against them, he remarks that they are a tribe of imitators, who can only describe what they have seen. And he fears that the Sophists, who are plentifully supplied with graces of speech, in their erratic way of life having never had a city or house of their own, may through want of experience err in their conception of philosophers and statesmen. 'And therefore to you I turn, Timaeus, citizen of Locris, who are at once a philosopher and a statesman, and to you, Critias, whom all Athenians know to be similarly accomplished, and to Hermocrates, who is also fitted by nature and education to share in our discourse.'

HERMOCRATES: 'We will do our best, and have been already preparing; for on our way home, Critias told us of an ancient tradition, which I wish, Critias, that you would repeat to Socrates.' 'I will, if

Timaeus approves.' 'I approve.' Listen then, Socrates, to a tale of Solon's, who, being the friend of Dropidas my great-grandfather, told it to my grandfather Critias, and he told me. The narrative related to ancient famous actions of the Athenian people, and to one especially, which I will rehearse in honour of you and of the goddess. Critias when he told this tale of the olden time, was ninety years old, I being not more than ten. The occasion of the rehearsal was the day of the Apaturia called the Registration of Youth, at which our parents gave prizes for recitation. Some poems of Solon were recited by the boys. They had not at that time gone out of fashion, and the recital of them led some one to say, perhaps in compliment to Critias, that Solon was not only the wisest of men but also the best of poets. The old man brightened up at hearing this, and said: Had Solon only had the leisure which was required to complete the famous legend which he brought with him from Egypt he would have been as distinguished as Homer and Hesiod. 'And what was the subject of the poem?' said the person who made the remark. The subject was a very noble one; he described the most famous action in which the Athenian people were ever engaged. But the memory of their exploits has passed away owing to the lapse of time and the extinction of the actors. 'Tell us,' said the other, 'the whole story, and where Solon heard the story.' He replied — There is at the head of the Egyptian Delta, where the river Nile divides, a city and district called Sais; the city was the birthplace of King Amasis, and is under the protection of the goddess Neith or Athene. The citizens have a friendly feeling towards the Athenians, believing themselves to be related to them. Hither came Solon, and was received with honour; and here he first learnt, by conversing with the Egyptian priests, how ignorant he and his countrymen were of antiquity. Perceiving this, and with the view of eliciting information from them, he told them the tales of Phoroneus and Niobe, and also of Deucalion and Pyrrha, and he endeavoured to count the generations which had since passed. Thereupon an aged priest said to him: 'O Solon, Solon, you Hellenes are ever young, and there is no old man who is a Hellene.' 'What do you mean?' he asked. 'In mind,' replied the priest, 'I mean to say that you are children; there is no opinion or tradition of knowledge among you which is white with age; and I will tell you why. Like the rest of mankind you have suffered from convulsions of nature, which are chiefly brought about by the two great agencies of fire and water. The former is symbolized in the Hellenic tale of young Phaethon who drove his father's horses the wrong way, and having burnt up the earth was himself burnt up by a thunderbolt. For there occurs at long intervals a derangement of the heavenly bodies, and then the earth is destroyed by fire. At such times, and when fire is the agent, those who dwell by rivers or on the seashore are safer than those who dwell upon high and dry places, who in their turn are safer when the danger is from water. Now the Nile is our saviour from fire, and as there is little rain in Egypt, we are not harmed by water; whereas in other countries, when a deluge comes, the inhabitants are swept by the rivers into the sea. The memorials which your own and other nations have once had of the famous actions of mankind perish in the waters at certain periods; and the rude survivors in the mountains begin again, knowing nothing of the world before the flood. But in Egypt the traditions of our own and other lands are by us registered for ever in our temples. The genealogies which you have recited to us out of your own annals, Solon, are a mere children's story. For in the first place, you remember one deluge only, and there were many of them, and you know nothing of that fairest and noblest race of which you are a seed or remnant. The memory of them was lost, because there was no written voice among you. For in the times before the great flood Athens was the greatest and best of cities and did the noblest deeds and had the best constitution of any under the face of heaven.' Solon marvelled, and desired to be informed of the particulars. 'You are welcome to hear them,' said the priest, 'both for your own sake and for that of the city, and above all for the sake of the goddess who is the common foundress of both our cities. Nine thousand years have elapsed since she founded yours, and eight thousand since she founded ours, as our annals record. Many laws exist among us which are the counterpart of yours as they were in the olden time. I will briefly describe them to you, and you shall read the account of them at your leisure in the sacred registers. In the first place, there was a caste of priests among the ancient Athenians, and another of artisans; also castes of shepherds, hunters, and husbandmen, and lastly of warriors, who, like the warriors of Egypt, were separated from the rest, and carried shields and spears, a custom which the goddess first taught you, and then the Asiatics, and we among Asiatics first received from her. Observe again, what care the law took in the pursuit of wisdom, searching out the deep things of the world, and applying them to the use of man. The spot of earth which the goddess chose had the best of climates, and produced the wisest men; in no other was she herself, the philosopher and warrior goddess, so likely to have votaries. And there you dwelt as became the children of the gods, excelling all men in virtue, and many famous actions are recorded of you. The most famous of them all was the overthrow of the island of Atlantis. This great island lay over against the Pillars of Heracles, in extent greater than Libya and Asia put together, and was the passage to other islands and to a great ocean of which the Mediterranean sea was only the harbour; and within the Pillars the empire of Atlantis reached in Europe to Tyrrhenia and in Libya to Egypt. This mighty power was arrayed against Egypt and Hellas and all the countries bordering on the Mediterranean. Then your city did bravely, and won renown over the whole earth. For at the peril of her own existence, and when the other Hellenes had deserted her, she repelled the invader, and of her own accord gave liberty to all the nations within the Pillars. A little while afterwards there were great earthquakes and floods, and your warrior race all sank into the earth; and the great island of Atlantis also disappeared in the sea. This is the explanation of the shallows which are found in that part of the Atlantic ocean.'

Such was the tale, Socrates, which Critias heard from Solon; and I noticed when listening to you yesterday, how close the resemblance was between your city and citizens and the ancient Athenian State. But I would not speak at the time, because I wanted to refresh my memory. I had heard the old man when I was a child, and though I could not remember the whole of our yesterday's discourse, I was able to recall every word of this, which is branded into my mind; and I am prepared, Socrates, to rehearse to you the entire narrative. The imaginary State which you were describing may be identified with the reality of Solon, and our antediluvian ancestors may be your citizens. 'That is excellent, Critias, and very appropriate to a Panathenaic festival; the truth of the story is a great advantage.' Then now let me explain to you the order of our entertainment; first, Timaeus, who is a natural philosopher, will speak of the origin of the world, going down to the creation of man, and then I shall receive the men whom he has created, and some of whom will have been educated by you, and introduce them to you as the lost Athenian citizens of whom the Egyptian record spoke. As the law of Solon prescribes, we will bring them into court and acknowledge their claims to citizenship. 'I see,' replied Socrates, 'that I shall be well entertained; and do you, Timaeus, offer up a prayer and begin.'

TIMAEUS: All men who have any right feeling, at the beginning of any enterprise, call upon the Gods; and he who is about to speak of the origin of the universe has a special need of their aid. May my words be acceptable to them, and may I speak in the manner which will be most intelligible to you and will best express my own meaning!

First, I must distinguish between that which always is and never becomes and which is apprehended by reason and reflection, and that which always becomes and never is and is conceived by opinion with the help of sense. All that becomes and is created is the work of a cause, and that is fair which the artificer makes after an eternal pattern, but whatever is fashioned after a created pattern is not fair. Is the world created or uncreated? — that is the first question. Created, I reply, being visible and tangible and having a body, and therefore sensible; and if sensible, then created; and if created, made by a cause, and the cause is the ineffable father of all things, who had before him an eternal archetype. For to imagine that the archetype was created would be blasphemy, seeing that the world is the noblest of creations, and God is the best of causes. And the world being thus created according to the eternal pattern is the copy of something; and we may assume that words are akin to the matter of which they speak. What is spoken of the unchanging or intelligible must be certain and true; but what is spoken of the created image can only be probable; being is to becoming what truth is to belief. And amid the variety of opinions which have arisen about God and the nature of the world we must be content to take probability for our rule, considering that I, who am the speaker, and you, who are the judges, are only men; to probability we may attain but no further.

SOCRATES: Excellent, Timaeus, I like your manner of approaching the subject — proceed.

TIMAEUS: Why did the Creator make the world? . . . He was good, and therefore not jealous, and being free from jealousy he desired that all things should be like himself. Wherefore he set in order the visible world, which he found in disorder. Now he who is the best could only create the fairest; and reflecting that of visible things the intelligent is superior to the unintelligent, he put intelligence in soul and soul in body, and framed the universe to be the best and fairest work in the order of nature, and the world became a living soul through the providence of God.

In the likeness of what animal was the world made? — that is the third question . . . The form of the perfect animal was a whole, and contained all intelligible beings, and the visible animal, made after the pattern of this, included all visible creatures.

Are there many worlds or one only? — that is the fourth question . . . One only. For if in the original there had been more than one they would have been the parts of a third, which would have been the true pattern of the world; and therefore there is, and will ever be, but one created world. Now that which is created is of necessity corporeal and visible and tangible — visible and therefore made of fire — tangible and therefore solid and made of earth. But two terms must be united by a third, which is a mean between them; and had the earth been a surface only, one mean would have sufficed, but two means are required to unite solid bodies. And as the world was composed of solids, between the elements of fire and earth God placed two other elements of air and water, and arranged them in a continuous proportion —

fire:air::air:water, and air:water::water:earth,

and so put together a visible and palpable heaven, having harmony and friendship in the union of the four elements; and being at unity with itself it was indissoluble except by the hand of the framer. Each of the elements was taken into the universe whole and entire; for he considered that the animal should be perfect and one, leaving no remnants out of which another animal could be created, and should also be free from old age and disease, which are produced by the action of external forces. And as he was to contain all things, he was made in the all-containing form of a sphere, round as from a lathe and every way equidistant from the centre, as was natural and suitable to him. He was finished and smooth, having neither eyes nor ears, for there was nothing without him which he could see or hear; and he had no need to carry food to his mouth, nor was there air for him to breathe; and he did not require hands, for there was nothing of which he could take hold, nor feet, with which to walk. All that he did was done rationally in and by himself, and he moved in a circle turning within himself, which is the most intellectual of motions; but the other six motions were wanting to him; wherefore the universe had no feet or legs.

And so the thought of God made a God in the image of a perfect body, having intercourse with himself and needing no other, but in every part harmonious and self-contained and truly blessed. The soul was first made by him — the elder to rule the younger; not in the order in which our wayward fancy has led us to describe them, but the soul first and afterwards the body. God took of the unchangeable and indivisible and also of the divisible and corporeal, and out of the two he made a third nature, essence, which was in a mean between them, and partook of the same and the other, the intractable nature of the other being compressed into the same. Having made a compound of all the three, he proceeded to divide the entire mass into portions related to one another in the ratios of 1, 2, 3, 4, 9, 8, 27, and proceeded to fill up the double and triple intervals thus —

— over 1, 4/3, 3/2, — over 2, 8/3, 3, — over 4, 16/3, 6, — over 8:— over 1, 3/2, 2, — over 3, 9/2, 6, — over 9, 27/2, 18, — over 27;

in which double series of numbers are two kinds of means; the one exceeds and is exceeded by equal parts of the extremes, e.g. 1, 4/3, 2; the other kind of mean is one which is equidistant from the extremes — 2, 4, 6. In this manner there were formed intervals of thirds, 3:2, of fourths, 4:3, and of ninths, 9:8. And next he filled up the intervals of a fourth with ninths, leaving a remnant which is in the ratio of 256:243. The entire compound was divided by him lengthways into two parts, which he united at the centre like the letter X, and bent into an inner and outer circle or sphere, cutting one another again at a point over against the point at which they cross. The outer circle or sphere was named the sphere of the same — the inner, the sphere of the other or diverse; and the one revolved horizontally to the right, the other diagonally to the left. To the sphere of the same which was undivided he gave dominion, but the sphere of the other or diverse was distributed into seven unequal orbits, having intervals in ratios of twos and threes, three of either sort, and he bade the orbits move in opposite directions to one another — three of them, the Sun, Mercury, Venus, with equal swiftness, and the remaining four — the Moon, Saturn, Mars, Jupiter, with unequal swiftness to the three and to one another, but all in due proportion.

When the Creator had made the soul he made the body within her; and the soul interfused everywhere from the centre to the circumference of heaven, herself turning in herself, began a divine life of rational and everlasting motion. The body of heaven is visible, but the soul is invisible, and partakes of reason and harmony, and is the best of creations, being the work of the best. And being composed of the same, the other, and the essence, these three, and also divided and bound in harmonical proportion, and revolving within herself — the soul when touching anything which has essence, whether divided or undivided, is stirred to utter the sameness or diversity of that and some other thing, and to tell how and when and where individuals are affected or related, whether in the world of change or of essence. When reason is in the neighbourhood of sense, and the circle of the other or diverse is moving truly, then arise true opinions and beliefs; when reason is in the sphere of thought, and the circle of the same runs smoothly, then intelligence is perfected.

When the Father who begat the world saw the image which he had made of the Eternal Gods moving and living, he rejoiced; and in his joy resolved, since the archetype was eternal, to make the creature eternal as far as this was possible. Wherefore he made an image of eternity which is time, having an uniform motion according to number, parted into months and days and years, and also having greater divisions of past, present, and future. These all apply to becoming in time, and have no meaning in relation to the eternal nature, which ever is and never was or will be; for the unchangeable is never older or younger, and when we say that he 'was' or 'will be,' we are mistaken, for these words are applicable only to becoming, and not to true being; and equally wrong are we in saying that what has become IS become and that what becomes IS becoming, and that the non-existent IS non- existent . . . These are the forms of time which imitate eternity and move in a circle measured by number.

Thus was time made in the image of the eternal nature; and it was created together with the heavens, in order that if they were dissolved, it might perish with them. And God made the sun and moon and five other wanderers, as they are called, seven in all, and to each of them he gave a body moving in an orbit, being one of the seven orbits into which the circle of the other was divided. He put the moon in the orbit which was nearest to the earth, the sun in that next, the morning star and Mercury in the orbits which move opposite to the sun but with equal swiftness — this being the reason why they overtake and are overtaken by one another. All these bodies became living creatures, and learnt their appointed tasks, and began to move, the nearer more swiftly, the remoter more slowly, according to the diagonal movement of the other. And since this was controlled by the movement of the same, the seven planets in their courses appeared to describe spirals; and that appeared fastest which was slowest, and that which overtook others appeared to be overtaken by them. And God lighted a fire in the second orbit from the earth which is called the sun, to give light over the whole heaven, and to teach intelligent beings that knowledge of number which is derived from the revolution of the same. Thus arose day and night, which are the periods of the most intelligent nature; a month is created by the revolution of the moon, a year by that of the sun. Other periods of wonderful length and complexity are not observed by men in general; there is moreover a cycle or perfect year at the completion of which they all meet and coincide . . . To this end the stars came into being, that the created heaven might imitate the eternal nature.

Thus far the universal animal was made in the divine image, but the other animals were not as yet included in him. And God created them according to the patterns or species of them which existed in the divine original. There are four of them: one of gods, another of birds, a third of fishes, and a fourth of animals. The gods were made in the form of a circle, which is the most perfect figure and the figure of the universe. They were created chiefly of fire, that they might be bright, and were made to know and follow the best, and to be scattered over the heavens, of which they were to be the glory. Two kinds of motion were assigned to them — first, the revolution in the same and around the same, in peaceful unchanging thought of the same; and to this was added a forward motion which was under the control of the same. Thus then the fixed stars were created, being divine and eternal animals, revolving on the same spot, and the wandering stars, in their courses, were created in the manner already described. The earth, which is our nurse, clinging around the pole extended through the universe, he made to be the guardian and artificer of night and day, first and eldest of gods that are in the interior of heaven. Vain would be the labour of telling all the figures of them, moving as in dance, and their juxta-positions and approximations, and when and where and behind what other stars they appear to disappear — to tell of all this without looking at a plan of them would be labour in vain.

The knowledge of the other gods is beyond us, and we can only accept the traditions of the ancients, who were the children of the gods, as they said; for surely they must have known their own ancestors. Although they give no proof, we must believe them as is customary. They tell us that Oceanus and Tethys were the children of Earth and Heaven; that Phoreys, Cronos, and Rhea came in the next generation, and were followed by Zeus and Here, whose brothers and children are known to everybody.

When all of them, both those who show themselves in the sky, and those who retire from view, had come into being, the Creator addressed them thus:— 'Gods, sons of gods, my works, if I will, are indissoluble. That which is bound may be dissolved, but only an evil being would dissolve that which is harmonious and happy. And although you are not immortal you shall not die, for I will hold you together. Hear me, then:— Three tribes of mortal beings have still to be created, but if created by me they would be like gods. Do ye therefore make them, I will implant in them the seed of immortality, and you shall weave together the mortal and immortal, and provide food for them, and receive them again in death.' Thus he spake, and poured the remains of the elements into the cup in which he had mingled the soul of the universe. They were no longer pure as before, but diluted; and the mixture he distributed into souls equal in number to the stars, and assigned each to a star — then having mounted them, as in a chariot, he showed them the nature of the universe, and told them of their future birth and human lot. They were to be sown in the planets, and out of them was to come forth the most religious of animals, which would hereafter be called man. The souls were to be implanted in bodies, which were in a perpetual flux, whence, he said, would arise, first, sensation; secondly, love, which is a mixture of pleasure and pain; thirdly, fear and anger, and the opposite affections: and if they conquered these, they would live righteously, but if they were conquered by them, unrighteously. He who lived well would return to his native star, and would there have a blessed existence; but, if he lived ill, he would pass into the nature of a woman, and if he did not then alter his evil ways, into the likeness of some animal, until the reason which was in him reasserted her sway over the elements of fire, air, earth, water, which had engrossed her, and he regained his first and better nature. Having given this law to his creatures, that he might be guiltless of their future evil, he sowed them, some in the earth, some in the moon, and some in the other planets; and he ordered the younger gods to frame human bodies for them and to make the necessary additions to them, and to avert from them all but self-inflicted evil.

Having given these commands, the Creator remained in his own nature. And his children, receiving from him the immortal principle, borrowed from the world portions of earth, air, fire, water, hereafter to be returned, which they fastened together, not with the adamantine bonds which bound themselves, but by little invisible pegs, making each separate body out of all the elements, subject to influx and efflux, and containing the courses of the soul. These swelling and surging as in a river moved irregularly and irrationally in all the six possible ways, forwards, backwards, right, left, up and down. But violent as were the internal and alimentary fluids, the tide became still more violent when the body came into contact with flaming fire, or the solid earth, or gliding waters, or the stormy wind; the motions produced by these impulses pass through the body to the soul and have the name of sensations. Uniting with the ever-flowing current, they shake the courses of the soul, stopping the revolution of the same and twisting in all sorts of ways the nature of the other, and the harmonical ratios of twos and threes and the mean terms which connect them, until the circles are bent and disordered and their motion becomes irregular. You may imagine a position of the body in which the head is resting upon the ground, and the legs are in the air, and the top is bottom and the left right. And something similar happens when the disordered motions of the soul come into contact with any external thing; they say the same or the other in a manner which is the very opposite of the truth, and they are false and foolish, and have no guiding principle in them. And when external impressions enter in, they are really conquered, though they seem to conquer.

By reason of these affections the soul is at first without intelligence, but as time goes on the stream of nutriment abates, and the courses of the soul regain their proper motion, and apprehend the same and the other rightly, and become rational. The soul of him who has education is whole and perfect and escapes the worst disease, but, if a man's education be neglected, he walks lamely through life and returns good for nothing to the world below. This, however, is an after-stage — at present, we are only concerned with the creation of the body and soul.

The two divine courses were encased by the gods in a sphere which is called the head, and is the god and lord of us. And to this they gave the body to be a vehicle, and the members to be instruments, having the power of flexion and extension. Such was the origin of legs and arms. In the next place, the gods gave a forward motion to the human body, because the front part of man was the more honourable and had authority. And they put in a face in which they inserted organs to minister in all things to the providence of the soul. They first contrived the eyes, into which they conveyed a light akin to the light of day, making it flow through the pupils. When the light of the eye is surrounded by the light of day, then like falls upon like, and they unite and form one body which conveys to the soul the motions of visible objects. But when the visual ray goes forth into the darkness, then unlike falls upon unlike — the eye no longer sees, and we go to sleep. The fire or light, when kept in by the eyelids, equalizes the inward motions, and there is rest accompanied by few dreams; only when the greater motions remain they engender in us corresponding visions of the night. And now we shall be able to understand the nature of reflections in mirrors. The fires from within and from without meet about the smooth and bright surface of the mirror; and because they meet in a manner contrary to the usual mode, the right and left sides of the object are transposed. In a concave mirror the top and bottom are inverted, but this is no transposition.

These are the second causes which God used as his ministers in fashioning the world. They are thought by many to be the prime causes, but they are not so; for they are destitute of mind and reason, and the lover of mind will not allow that there are any prime causes other than the rational and invisible ones — these he investigates first, and afterwards the causes of things which are moved by others, and which work by chance and without order. Of the second or concurrent causes of sight I have already spoken, and I will now speak of the higher purpose of God in giving us eyes. Sight is the source of the greatest benefits to us; for if our eyes had never seen the sun, stars, and heavens, the words which we have spoken would not have been uttered. The sight of them and their revolutions has given us the knowledge of number and time, the power of enquiry, and philosophy, which is the great blessing of human life; not to speak of the lesser benefits which even the vulgar can appreciate. God gave us the faculty of sight that we might behold the order of the heavens and create a corresponding order in our own erring minds. To the like end the gifts of speech and hearing were bestowed upon us; not for the sake of irrational pleasure, but in order that we might harmonize the courses of the soul by sympathy with the harmony of sound, and cure ourselves of our irregular and graceless ways.

Thus far we have spoken of the works of mind; and there are other works done from necessity, which we must now place beside them; for the creation is made up of both, mind persuading necessity as far as possible to work out good. Before the heavens there existed fire, air, water, earth, which we suppose men to know, though no one has explained their nature, and we erroneously maintain them to be the letters or elements of the whole, although they cannot reasonably be compared even to syllables or first compounds. I am not now speaking of the first principles of things, because I cannot discover them by our present mode of enquiry. But as I observed the rule of probability at first, I will begin anew, seeking by the grace of God to observe it still.

In our former discussion I distinguished two kinds of being — the unchanging or invisible, and the visible or changing. But now a third kind is required, which I shall call the receptacle or nurse of generation. There is a difficulty in arriving at an exact notion of this third kind, because the four elements themselves are of inexact natures and easily pass into one another, and are too transient to be detained by any one name; wherefore we are compelled to speak of water or fire, not as substances, but as qualities. They may be compared to images made of gold, which are continually assuming new forms. Somebody asks what they are; if you do not know, the safest answer is to reply that they are gold. In like manner there is a universal nature out of which all things are made, and which is like none of them; but they enter into and pass out of her, and are made after patterns of the true in a wonderful and inexplicable manner. The containing principle may be likened to a mother, the source or spring to a father, the intermediate nature to a child; and we may also remark that the matter which receives every variety of form must be formless, like the inodorous liquids which are prepared to receive scents, or the smooth and soft materials on which figures are impressed. In the same way space or matter is neither earth nor fire nor air nor water, but an invisible and formless being which receives all things, and in an incomprehensible manner partakes of the intelligible. But we may say, speaking generally, that fire is that part of this nature which is inflamed, water that which is moistened, and the like.

Let me ask a question in which a great principle is involved: Is there an essence of fire and the other elements, or are there only fires visible to sense? I answer in a word: If mind is one thing and true opinion another, then there are self-existent essences; but if mind is the same with opinion, then the visible and corporeal is most real. But they are not the same, and they have a different origin and nature. The one comes to us by instruction, the other by persuasion, the one is rational, the other is irrational, the one is movable by persuasion, the other immovable; the one is possessed by every man, the other by the gods and by very few men. And we must acknowledge that as there are two kinds of knowledge, so there are two kinds of being corresponding to them; the one uncreated, indestructible, immovable, which is seen by intelligence only; the other created, which is always becoming in place and vanishing out of place, and is apprehended by opinion and sense. There is also a third nature — that of space, which is indestructible, and is perceived by a kind of spurious reason without the help of sense. This is presented to us in a dreamy manner, and yet is said to be necessary, for we say that all things must be somewhere in space. For they are the images of other things and must therefore have a separate existence and exist in something (i.e. in space). But true reason assures us that while two things (i.e. the idea and the image) are different they cannot inhere in one another, so as to be one and two at the same time.

To sum up: Being and generation and space, these three, existed before the heavens, and the nurse or vessel of generation, moistened by water and inflamed by fire, and taking the forms of air and earth, assumed various shapes. By the motion of the vessel, the elements were divided, and like grain winnowed by fans, the close and heavy particles settled in one place, the light and airy ones in another. At first they were without reason and measure, and had only certain faint traces of themselves, until God fashioned them by figure and number. In this, as in every other part of creation, I suppose God to have made things, as far as was possible, fair and good, out of things not fair and good.

And now I will explain to you the generation of the world by a method with which your scientific training will have made you familiar. Fire, air, earth, and water are bodies and therefore solids, and solids are contained in planes, and plane rectilinear figures are made up of triangles. Of triangles there are two kinds; one having the opposite sides equal (isosceles), the other with unequal sides (scalene). These we may fairly assume to be the original elements of fire and the other bodies; what principles are prior to these God only knows, and he of men whom God loves. Next, we must determine what are the four most beautiful figures which are unlike one another and yet sometimes capable of resolution into one another . . . Of the two kinds of triangles the equal-sided has but one form, the unequal-sided has an infinite variety of forms; and there is none more beautiful than that which forms the half of an equilateral triangle. Let us then choose two triangles; one, the isosceles, the other, that form of scalene which has the square of the longer side three times as great as the square of the lesser side; and affirm that, out of these, fire and the other elements have been constructed.

I was wrong in imagining that all the four elements could be generated into and out of one another. For as they are formed, three of them from the triangle which has the sides unequal, the fourth from the triangle which has equal sides, three can be resolved into one another, but the fourth cannot be resolved into them nor they into it. So much for their passage into one another: I must now speak of their construction. From the triangle of which the hypotenuse is twice the lesser side the three first regular solids are formed — first, the equilateral pyramid or tetrahedron; secondly, the octahedron; thirdly, the icosahedron; and from the isosceles triangle is formed the cube. And there is a fifth figure (which is made out of twelve pentagons), the dodecahedron — this God used as a model for the twelvefold division of the Zodiac.

Let us now assign the geometrical forms to their respective elements. The cube is the most stable of them because resting on a quadrangular plane surface, and composed of isosceles triangles. To the earth then, which is the most stable of bodies and the most easily modelled of them, may be assigned the form of a cube; and the remaining forms to the other elements — to fire the pyramid, to air the octahedron, and to water the icosahedron — according to their degrees of lightness or heaviness or power, or want of power, of penetration. The single particles of any of the elements are not seen by reason of their smallness; they only become visible when collected. The ratios of their motions, numbers, and other properties, are ordered by the God, who harmonized them as far as necessity permitted.

The probable conclusion is as follows:— Earth, when dissolved by the more penetrating element of fire, whether acting immediately or through the medium of air or water, is decomposed but not transformed. Water, when divided by fire or air, becomes one part fire, and two parts air. A volume of air divided becomes two of fire. On the other hand, when condensed, two volumes of fire make a volume of air; and two and a half parts of air condense into one of water. Any element which is fastened upon by fire is cut by the sharpness of the triangles, until at length, coalescing with the fire, it is at rest; for similars are not affected by similars. When two kinds of bodies quarrel with one another, then the tendency to decomposition continues until the smaller either escapes to its kindred element or becomes one with its conqueror. And this tendency in bodies to condense or escape is a source of motion . . . Where there is motion there must be a mover, and where there is a mover there must be something to move. These cannot exist in what is uniform, and therefore motion is due to want of uniformity. But then why, when things are divided after their kinds, do they not cease from motion? The answer is, that the circular motion of all things compresses them, and as 'nature abhors a vacuum,' the finer and more subtle particles of the lighter elements, such as fire and air, are thrust into the interstices of the larger, each of them penetrating according to their rarity, and thus all the elements are on their way up and down everywhere and always into their own places. Hence there is a principle of inequality, and therefore of motion, in all time.

In the next place, we may observe that there are different kinds of fire — (1) flame, (2) light that burns not, (3) the red heat of the embers of fire. And there are varieties of air, as for example, the pure aether, the opaque mist, and other nameless forms. Water, again, is of two kinds, liquid and fusile. The liquid is composed of small and unequal particles, the fusile of large and uniform particles and is more solid, but nevertheless melts at the approach of fire, and then spreads upon the earth. When the substance cools, the fire passes into the air, which is displaced, and forces together and condenses the liquid mass. This process is called cooling and congealment. Of the fusile kinds the fairest and heaviest is gold; this is hardened by filtration through rock, and is of a bright yellow colour. A shoot of gold which is darker and denser than the rest is called adamant. Another kind is called copper, which is harder and yet lighter because the interstices are larger than in gold. There is mingled with it a fine and small portion of earth which comes out in the form of rust. These are a few of the conjectures which philosophy forms, when, leaving the eternal nature, she turns for innocent recreation to consider the truths of generation.

Water which is mingled with fire is called liquid because it rolls upon the earth, and soft because its bases give way. This becomes more equable when separated from fire and air, and then congeals into hail or ice, or the looser forms of hoar frost or snow. There are other waters which are called juices and are distilled through plants. Of these we may mention, first, wine, which warms the soul as well as the body; secondly, oily substances, as for example, oil or pitch; thirdly, honey, which relaxes the contracted parts of the mouth and so produces sweetness; fourthly, vegetable acid, which is frothy and has a burning quality and dissolves the flesh. Of the kinds of earth, that which is filtered through water passes into stone; the water is broken up by the earth and escapes in the form of air — this in turn presses upon the mass of earth, and the earth, compressed into an indissoluble union with the remaining water, becomes rock. Rock, when it is made up of equal particles, is fair and transparent, but the reverse when of unequal. Earth is converted into pottery when the watery part is suddenly drawn away; or if moisture remains, the earth, when fused by fire, becomes, on cooling, a stone of a black colour. When the earth is finer and of a briny nature then two half-solid bodies are formed by separating the water — soda and salt. The strong compounds of earth and water are not soluble by water, but only by fire. Earth itself, when not consolidated, is dissolved by water; when consolidated, by fire only. The cohesion of water, when strong, is dissolved by fire only; when weak, either by air or fire, the former entering the interstices, the latter penetrating even the triangles. Air when strongly condensed is indissoluble by any power which does not reach the triangles, and even when not strongly condensed is only resolved by fire. Compounds of earth and water are unaffected by water while the water occupies the interstices in them, but begin to liquefy when fire enters into the interstices of the water. They are of two kinds, some of them, like glass, having more earth, others, like wax, having more water in them.

Having considered objects of sense, we now pass on to sensation. But we cannot explain sensation without explaining the nature of flesh and of the mortal soul; and as we cannot treat of both together, in order that we may proceed at once to the sensations we must assume the existence of body and soul.

What makes fire burn? The fineness of the sides, the sharpness of the angles, the smallness of the particles, the quickness of the motion. Moreover, the pyramid, which is the figure of fire, is more cutting than any other. The feeling of cold is produced by the larger particles of moisture outside the body trying to eject the smaller ones in the body which they compress. The struggle which arises between elements thus unnaturally brought together causes shivering. That is hard to which the flesh yields, and soft which yields to the flesh, and these two terms are also relative to one another. The yielding matter is that which has the slenderest base, whereas that which has a rectangular base is compact and repellent. Light and heavy are wrongly explained with reference to a lower and higher in place. For in the universe, which is a sphere, there is no opposition of above or below, and that which is to us above would be below to a man standing at the antipodes. The greater or less difficulty in detaching any element from its like is the real cause of heaviness or of lightness. If you draw the earth into the dissimilar air, the particles of earth cling to their native element, and you more easily detach a small portion than a large. There would be the same difficulty in moving any of the upper elements towards the lower. The smooth and the rough are severally produced by the union of evenness with compactness, and of hardness with inequality.

Pleasure and pain are the most important of the affections common to the whole body. According to our general doctrine of sensation, parts of the body which are easily moved readily transmit the motion to the mind; but parts which are not easily moved have no effect upon the patient. The bones and hair are of the latter kind, sight and hearing of the former. Ordinary affections are neither pleasant nor painful. The impressions of sight afford an example of these, and are neither violent nor sudden. But sudden replenishments of the body cause pleasure, and sudden disturbances, as for example cuttings and burnings, have the opposite effect.

>From sensations common to the whole body, we proceed to those of particular parts. The affections of the tongue appear to be caused by contraction and dilation, but they have more of roughness or smoothness than is found in other affections. Earthy particles, entering into the small veins of the tongue which reach to the heart, when they melt into and dry up the little veins are astringent if they are rough; or if not so rough, they are only harsh, and if excessively abstergent, like potash and soda, bitter. Purgatives of a weaker sort are called salt and, having no bitterness, are rather agreeable. Inflammatory bodies, which by their lightness are carried up into the head, cutting all that comes in their way, are termed pungent. But when these are refined by putrefaction, and enter the narrow veins of the tongue, and meet there particles of earth and air, two kinds of globules are formed — one of earthy and impure liquid, which boils and ferments, the other of pure and transparent water, which are called bubbles; of all these affections the cause is termed acid. When, on the other hand, the composition of the deliquescent particles is congenial to the tongue, and disposes the parts according to their nature, this remedial power in them is called sweet.

Smells are not divided into kinds; all of them are transitional, and arise out of the decomposition of one element into another, for the simple air or water is without smell. They are vapours or mists, thinner than water and thicker than air: and hence in drawing in the breath, when there is an obstruction, the air passes, but there is no smell. They have no names, but are distinguished as pleasant and unpleasant, and their influence extends over the whole region from the head to the navel.

Hearing is the effect of a stroke which is transmitted through the ears by means of the air, brain, and blood to the soul, beginning at the head and extending to the liver. The sound which moves swiftly is acute; that which moves slowly is grave; that which is uniform is smooth, and the opposite is harsh. Loudness depends on the quantity of the sound. Of the harmony of sounds I will hereafter speak.

Colours are flames which emanate from all bodies, having particles corresponding to the sense of sight. Some of the particles are less and some larger, and some are equal to the parts of the sight. The equal particles appear transparent; the larger contract, and the lesser dilate the sight. White is produced by the dilation, black by the contraction, of the particles of sight. There is also a swifter motion of another sort of fire which forces a way through the passages of the eyes, and elicits from them a union of fire and water which we call tears. The inner fire flashes forth, and the outer finds a way in and is extinguished in the moisture, and all sorts of colours are generated by the mixture. This affection is termed by us dazzling, and the object which produces it is called bright. There is yet another sort of fire which mingles with the moisture of the eye without flashing, and produces a colour like blood — to this we give the name of red.

A bright element mingling with red and white produces a colour which we call auburn. The law of proportion, however, according to which compound colours are formed, cannot be determined scientifically or even probably. Red, when mingled with black and white, gives a purple hue, which becomes umber when the colours are burnt and there is a larger admixture of black. Flame-colour is a mixture of auburn and dun; dun of white and black; yellow of white and auburn. White and bright meeting, and falling upon a full black, become dark blue; dark blue mingling with white becomes a light blue; the union of flame-colour and black makes leek-green. There is no difficulty in seeing how other colours are probably composed. But he who should attempt to test the truth of this by experiment, would forget the difference of the human and divine nature. God only is able to compound and resolve substances; such experiments are impossible to man.

These are the elements of necessity which the Creator received in the world of generation when he made the all-sufficient and perfect creature, using the secondary causes as his ministers, but himself fashioning the good in all things. For there are two sorts of causes, the one divine, the other necessary; and we should seek to discover the divine above all, and, for their sake, the necessary, because without them the higher cannot be attained by us.

Having now before us the causes out of which the rest of our discourse is to be framed, let us go back to the point at which we began, and add a fair ending to our tale. As I said at first, all things were originally a chaos in which there was no order or proportion. The elements of this chaos were arranged by the Creator, and out of them he made the world. Of the divine he himself was the author, but he committed to his offspring the creation of the mortal. From him they received the immortal soul, but themselves made the body to be its vehicle, and constructed within another soul which was mortal, and subject to terrible affections — pleasure, the inciter of evil; pain, which deters from good; rashness and fear, foolish counsellors; anger hard to be appeased; hope easily led astray. These they mingled with irrational sense and all-daring love according to necessary laws and so framed man. And, fearing to pollute the divine element, they gave the mortal soul a separate habitation in the breast, parted off from the head by a narrow isthmus. And as in a house the women's apartments are divided from the men's, the cavity of the thorax was divided into two parts, a higher and a lower. The higher of the two, which is the seat of courage and anger, lies nearer to the head, between the midriff and the neck, and assists reason in restraining the desires. The heart is the house of guard in which all the veins meet, and through them reason sends her commands to the extremity of her kingdom. When the passions are in revolt, or danger approaches from without, then the heart beats and swells; and the creating powers, knowing this, implanted in the body the soft and bloodless substance of the lung, having a porous and springy nature like a sponge, and being kept cool by drink and air which enters through the trachea.

The part of the soul which desires meat and drink was placed between the midriff and navel, where they made a sort of manger; and here they bound it down, like a wild animal, away from the council-chamber, and leaving the better principle undisturbed to advise quietly for the good of the whole. For the Creator knew that the belly would not listen to reason, and was under the power of idols and fancies. Wherefore he framed the liver to connect with the lower nature, contriving that it should be compact, and bright, and sweet, and also bitter and smooth, in order that the power of thought which originates in the mind might there be reflected, terrifying the belly with the elements of bitterness and gall, and a suffusion of bilious colours when the liver is contracted, and causing pain and misery by twisting out of its place the lobe and closing up the vessels and gates. And the converse happens when some gentle inspiration coming from intelligence mirrors the opposite fancies, giving rest and sweetness and freedom, and at night, moderation and peace accompanied with prophetic insight, when reason and sense are asleep. For the authors of our being, in obedience to their Father's will and in order to make men as good as they could, gave to the liver the power of divination, which is never active when men are awake or in health; but when they are under the influence of some disorder or enthusiasm then they receive intimations, which have to be interpreted by others who are called prophets, but should rather be called interpreters of prophecy; after death these intimations become unintelligible. The spleen which is situated in the neighbourhood, on the left side, keeps the liver bright and clean, as a napkin does a mirror, and the evacuations of the liver are received into it; and being a hollow tissue it is for a time swollen with these impurities, but when the body is purged it returns to its natural size.

The truth concerning the soul can only be established by the word of God. Still, we may venture to assert what is probable both concerning soul and body.

The creative powers were aware of our tendency to excess. And so when they made the belly to be a receptacle for food, in order that men might not perish by insatiable gluttony, they formed the convolutions of the intestines, in this way retarding the passage of food through the body, lest mankind should be absorbed in eating and drinking, and the whole race become impervious to divine philosophy.

The creation of bones and flesh was on this wise. The foundation of these is the marrow which binds together body and soul, and the marrow is made out of such of the primary triangles as are adapted by their perfection to produce all the four elements. These God took and mingled them in due proportion, making as many kinds of marrow as there were hereafter to be kinds of souls. The receptacle of the divine soul he made round, and called that portion of the marrow brain, intending that the vessel containing this substance should be the head. The remaining part he divided into long and round figures, and to these as to anchors, fastening the mortal soul, he proceeded to make the rest of the body, first forming for both parts a covering of bone. The bone was formed by sifting pure smooth earth and wetting it with marrow. It was then thrust alternately into fire and water, and thus rendered insoluble by either. Of bone he made a globe which he placed around the brain, leaving a narrow opening, and around the marrow of the neck and spine he formed the vertebrae, like hinges, which extended from the head through the whole of the trunk. And as the bone was brittle and liable to mortify and destroy the marrow by too great rigidity and susceptibility to heat and cold, he contrived sinews and flesh — the first to give flexibility, the second to guard against heat and cold, and to be a protection against falls, containing a warm moisture, which in summer exudes and cools the body, and in winter is a defence against cold. Having this in view, the Creator mingled earth with fire and water and mixed with them a ferment of acid and salt, so as to form pulpy flesh. But the sinews he made of a mixture of bone and unfermented flesh, giving them a mean nature between the two, and a yellow colour. Hence they were more glutinous than flesh, but softer than bone. The bones which have most of the living soul within them he covered with the thinnest film of flesh, those which have least of it, he lodged deeper. At the joints he diminished the flesh in order not to impede the flexure of the limbs, and also to avoid clogging the perceptions of the mind. About the thighs and arms, which have no sense because there is little soul in the marrow, and about the inner bones, he laid the flesh thicker. For where the flesh is thicker there is less feeling, except in certain parts which the Creator has made solely of flesh, as for example, the tongue. Had the combination of solid bone and thick flesh been consistent with acute perceptions, the Creator would have given man a sinewy and fleshy head, and then he would have lived twice as long. But our creators were of opinion that a shorter life which was better was preferable to a longer which was worse, and therefore they covered the head with thin bone, and placed the sinews at the extremity of the head round the neck, and fastened the jawbones to them below the face. And they framed the mouth, having teeth and tongue and lips, with a view to the necessary and the good; for food is a necessity, and the river of speech is the best of rivers. Still, the head could not be left a bare globe of bone on account of the extremes of heat and cold, nor be allowed to become dull and senseless by an overgrowth of flesh. Wherefore it was covered by a peel or skin which met and grew by the help of the cerebral humour. The diversity of the sutures was caused by the struggle of the food against the courses of the soul. The skin of the head was pierced by fire, and out of the punctures came forth a moisture, part liquid, and part of a skinny nature, which was hardened by the pressure of the external cold and became hair. And God gave hair to the head of man to be a light covering, so that it might not interfere with his perceptions. Nails were formed by combining sinew, skin, and bone, and were made by the creators with a view to the future when, as they knew, women and other animals who would require them would be framed out of man.

The gods also mingled natures akin to that of man with other forms and perceptions. Thus trees and plants were created, which were originally wild and have been adapted by cultivation to our use. They partake of that third kind of life which is seated between the midriff and the navel, and is altogether passive and incapable of reflection.

When the creators had furnished all these natures for our sustenance, they cut channels through our bodies as in a garden, watering them with a perennial stream. Two were cut down the back, along the back bone, where the skin and flesh meet, one on the right and the other on the left, having the marrow of generation between them. In the next place, they divided the veins about the head and interlaced them with each other in order that they might form an additional link between the head and the body, and that the sensations from both sides might be diffused throughout the body. In the third place, they contrived the passage of liquids, which may be explained in this way:— Finer bodies retain coarser, but not the coarser the finer, and the belly is capable of retaining food, but not fire and air. God therefore formed a network of fire and air to irrigate the veins, having within it two lesser nets, and stretched cords reaching from both the lesser nets to the extremity of the outer net. The inner parts of the net were made by him of fire, the lesser nets and their cavities of air. The two latter he made to pass into the mouth; the one ascending by the air-pipes from the lungs, the other by the side of the air-pipes from the belly. The entrance to the first he divided into two parts, both of which he made to meet at the channels of the nose, that when the mouth was closed the passage connected with it might still be fed with air. The cavity of the network he spread around the hollows of the body, making the entire receptacle to flow into and out of the lesser nets and the lesser nets into and out of it, while the outer net found a way into and out of the pores of the body, and the internal heat followed the air to and fro. These, as we affirm, are the phenomena of respiration. And all this process takes place in order that the body may be watered and cooled and nourished, and the meat and drink digested and liquefied and carried into the veins.

The causes of respiration have now to be considered. The exhalation of the breath through the mouth and nostrils displaces the external air, and at the same time leaves a vacuum into which through the pores the air which is displaced enters. Also the vacuum which is made when the air is exhaled through the pores is filled up by the inhalation of breath through the mouth and nostrils. The explanation of this double phenomenon is as follows:— Elements move towards their natural places. Now as every animal has within him a fountain of fire, the air which is inhaled through the mouth and nostrils, on coming into contact with this, is heated; and when heated, in accordance with the law of attraction, it escapes by the way it entered toward the place of fire. On leaving the body it is cooled and drives round the air which it displaces through the pores into the empty lungs. This again is in turn heated by the internal fire and escapes, as it entered, through the pores.

The phenomena of medical cupping-glasses, of swallowing, and of the hurling of bodies, are to be explained on a similar principle; as also sounds, which are sometimes discordant on account of the inequality of them, and again harmonious by reason of equality. The slower sounds reaching the swifter, when they begin to pause, by degrees assimilate with them: whence arises a pleasure which even the unwise feel, and which to the wise becomes a higher sense of delight, being an imitation of divine harmony in mortal motions. Streams flow, lightnings play, amber and the magnet attract, not by reason of attraction, but because 'nature abhors a vacuum,' and because things, when compounded or dissolved, move different ways, each to its own place.

I will now return to the phenomena of respiration. The fire, entering the belly, minces the food, and as it escapes, fills the veins by drawing after it the divided portions, and thus the streams of nutriment are diffused through the body. The fruits or herbs which are our daily sustenance take all sorts of colours when intermixed, but the colour of red or fire predominates, and hence the liquid which we call blood is red, being the nurturing principle of the body, whence all parts are watered and empty places filled.

The process of repletion and depletion is produced by the attraction of like to like, after the manner of the universal motion. The external elements by their attraction are always diminishing the substance of the body: the particles of blood, too, formed out of the newly digested food, are attracted towards kindred elements within the body and so fill up the void. When more is taken away than flows in, then we decay; and when less, we grow and increase.

The young of every animal has the triangles new and closely locked together, and yet the entire frame is soft and delicate, being newly made of marrow and nurtured on milk. These triangles are sharper than those which enter the body from without in the shape of food, and therefore they cut them up. But as life advances, the triangles wear out and are no longer able to assimilate food; and at length, when the bonds which unite the triangles of the marrow become undone, they in turn unloose the bonds of the soul; and if the release be according to nature, she then flies away with joy. For the death which is natural is pleasant, but that which is caused by violence is painful.

Every one may understand the origin of diseases. They may be occasioned by the disarrangement or disproportion of the elements out of which the body is framed. This is the origin of many of them, but the worst of all owe their severity to the following causes: There is a natural order in the human frame according to which the flesh and sinews are made of blood, the sinews out of the fibres, and the flesh out of the congealed substance which is formed by separation from the fibres. The glutinous matter which comes away from the sinews and the flesh, not only binds the flesh to the bones, but nourishes the bones and waters the marrow. When these processes take place in regular order the body is in health.

But when the flesh wastes and returns into the veins there is discoloured blood as well as air in the veins, having acid and salt qualities, from which is generated every sort of phlegm and bile. All things go the wrong way and cease to give nourishment to the body, no longer preserving their natural courses, but at war with themselves and destructive to the constitution of the body. The oldest part of the flesh which is hard to decompose blackens from long burning, and from being corroded grows bitter, and as the bitter element refines away, becomes acid. When tinged with blood the bitter substance has a red colour, and this when mixed with black takes the hue of grass; or again, the bitter substance has an auburn colour, when new flesh is decomposed by the internal flame. To all which phenomena some physician or philosopher who was able to see the one in many has given the name of bile. The various kinds of bile have names answering to their colours. Lymph or serum is of two kinds: first, the whey of blood, which is gentle; secondly, the secretion of dark and bitter bile, which, when mingled under the influence of heat with salt, is malignant and is called acid phlegm. There is also white phlegm, formed by the decomposition of young and tender flesh, and covered with little bubbles, separately invisible, but becoming visible when collected. The water of tears and perspiration and similar substances is also the watery part of fresh phlegm. All these humours become sources of disease when the blood is replenished in irregular ways and not by food or drink. The danger, however, is not so great when the foundation remains, for then there is a possibility of recovery. But when the substance which unites the flesh and bones is diseased, and is no longer renewed from the muscles and sinews, and instead of being oily and smooth and glutinous becomes rough and salt and dry, then the fleshy parts fall away and leave the sinews bare and full of brine, and the flesh gets back again into the circulation of the blood, and makes the previously mentioned disorders still greater. There are other and worse diseases which are prior to these; as when the bone through the density of the flesh does not receive sufficient air, and becomes stagnant and gangrened, and crumbling away passes into the food, and the food into the flesh, and the flesh returns again into the blood. Worst of all and most fatal is the disease of the marrow, by which the whole course of the body is reversed. There is a third class of diseases which are produced, some by wind and some by phlegm and some by bile. When the lung, which is the steward of the air, is obstructed, by rheums, and in one part no air, and in another too much, enters in, then the parts which are unrefreshed by air corrode, and other parts are distorted by the excess of air; and in this manner painful diseases are produced. The most painful are caused by wind generated within the body, which gets about the great sinews of the shoulders — these are termed tetanus. The cure of them is difficult, and in most cases they are relieved only by fever. White phlegm, which is dangerous if kept in, by reason of the air bubbles, is not equally dangerous if able to escape through the pores, although it variegates the body, generating diverse kinds of leprosies. If, when mingled with black bile, it disturbs the courses of the head in sleep, there is not so much danger; but if it assails those who are awake, then the attack is far more dangerous, and is called epilepsy or the sacred disease. Acid and salt phlegm is the source of catarrh.

Inflammations originate in bile, which is sometimes relieved by boils and swellings, but when detained, and above all when mingled with pure blood, generates many inflammatory disorders, disturbing the position of the fibres which are scattered about in the blood in order to maintain the balance of rare and dense which is necessary to its regular circulation. If the bile, which is only stale blood, or liquefied flesh, comes in little by little, it is congealed by the fibres and produces internal cold and shuddering. But when it enters with more of a flood it overcomes the fibres by its heat and reaches the spinal marrow, and burning up the cables of the soul sets her free from the body. When on the other hand the body, though wasted, still holds out, then the bile is expelled, like an exile from a factious state, causing associating diarrhoeas and dysenteries and similar disorders. The body which is diseased from the effects of fire is in a continual fever; when air is the agent, the fever is quotidian; when water, the fever intermits a day; when earth, which is the most sluggish element, the fever intermits three days and is with difficulty shaken off.

Of mental disorders there are two sorts, one madness, the other ignorance, and they may be justly attributed to disease. Excessive pleasures or pains are among the greatest diseases, and deprive men of their senses. When the seed about the spinal marrow is too abundant, the body has too great pleasures and pains; and during a great part of his life he who is the subject of them is more or less mad. He is often thought bad, but this is a mistake; for the truth is that the intemperance of lust is due to the fluidity of the marrow produced by the loose consistency of the bones. And this is true of vice in general, which is commonly regarded as disgraceful, whereas it is really involuntary and arises from a bad habit of the body and evil education. In like manner the soul is often made vicious by the influence of bodily pain; the briny phlegm and other bitter and bilious humours wander over the body and find no exit, but are compressed within, and mingle their own vapours with the motions of the soul, and are carried to the three places of the soul, creating infinite varieties of trouble and melancholy, of rashness and cowardice, of forgetfulness and stupidity. When men are in this evil plight of body, and evil forms of government and evil discourses are superadded, and there is no education to save them, they are corrupted through two causes; but of neither of them are they really the authors. For the planters are to blame rather than the plants, the educators and not the educated. Still, we should endeavour to attain virtue and avoid vice; but this is part of another subject.

Enough of disease — I have now to speak of the means by which the mind and body are to be preserved, a higher theme than the other. The good is the beautiful, and the beautiful is the symmetrical, and there is no greater or fairer symmetry than that of body and soul, as the contrary is the greatest of deformities. A leg or an arm too long or too short is at once ugly and unserviceable, and the same is true if body and soul are disproportionate. For a strong and impassioned soul may 'fret the pigmy body to decay,' and so produce convulsions and other evils. The violence of controversy, or the earnestness of enquiry, will often generate inflammations and rheums which are not understood, or assigned to their true cause by the professors of medicine. And in like manner the body may be too much for the soul, darkening the reason, and quickening the animal desires. The only security is to preserve the balance of the two, and to this end the mathematician or philosopher must practise gymnastics, and the gymnast must cultivate music. The parts of the body too must be treated in the same way — they should receive their appropriate exercise. For the body is set in motion when it is heated and cooled by the elements which enter in, or is dried up and moistened by external things; and, if given up to these processes when at rest, it is liable to destruction. But the natural motion, as in the world, so also in the human frame, produces harmony and divides hostile powers. The best exercise is the spontaneous motion of the body, as in gymnastics, because most akin to the motion of mind; not so good is the motion of which the source is in another, as in sailing or riding; least good when the body is at rest and the motion is in parts only, which is a species of motion imparted by physic. This should only be resorted to by men of sense in extreme cases; lesser diseases are not to be irritated by medicine. For every disease is akin to the living being and has an appointed term, just as life has, which depends on the form of the triangles, and cannot be protracted when they are worn out. And he who, instead of accepting his destiny, endeavours to prolong his life by medicine, is likely to multiply and magnify his diseases. Regimen and not medicine is the true cure, when a man has time at his disposal.

Enough of the nature of man and of the body, and of training and education. The subject is a great one and cannot be adequately treated as an appendage to another. To sum up all in a word: there are three kinds of soul located within us, and any one of them, if remaining inactive, becomes very weak; if exercised, very strong. Wherefore we should duly train and exercise all three kinds.

The divine soul God lodged in the head, to raise us, like plants which are not of earthly origin, to our kindred; for the head is nearest to heaven. He who is intent upon the gratification of his desires and cherishes the mortal soul, has all his ideas mortal, and is himself mortal in the truest sense. But he who seeks after knowledge and exercises the divine part of himself in godly and immortal thoughts, attains to truth and immortality, as far as is possible to man, and also to happiness, while he is training up within him the divine principle and indwelling power of order. There is only one way in which one person can benefit another; and that is by assigning to him his proper nurture and motion. To the motions of the soul answer the motions of the universe, and by the study of these the individual is restored to his original nature.

Thus we have finished the discussion of the universe, which, according to our original intention, has now been brought down to the creation of man. Completeness seems to require that something should be briefly said about other animals: first of women, who are probably degenerate and cowardly men. And when they degenerated, the gods implanted in men the desire of union with them, creating in man one animate substance and in woman another in the following manner:— The outlet for liquids they connected with the living principle of the spinal marrow, which the man has the desire to emit into the fruitful womb of the woman; this is like a fertile field in which the seed is quickened and matured, and at last brought to light. When this desire is unsatisfied the man is over-mastered by the power of the generative organs, and the woman is subjected to disorders from the obstruction of the passages of the breath, until the two meet and pluck the fruit of the tree.

The race of birds was created out of innocent, light-minded men, who thought to pursue the study of the heavens by sight; these were transformed into birds, and grew feathers instead of hair. The race of wild animals were men who had no philosophy, and never looked up to heaven or used the courses of the head, but followed only the influences of passion. Naturally they turned to their kindred earth, and put their forelegs to the ground, and their heads were crushed into strange oblong forms. Some of them have four feet, and some of them more than four — the latter, who are the more senseless, drawing closer to their native element; the most senseless of all have no limbs and trail their whole body on the ground. The fourth kind are the inhabitants of the waters; these are made out of the most senseless and ignorant and impure of men, whom God placed in the uttermost parts of the world in return for their utter ignorance, and caused them to respire water instead of the pure element of air. Such are the laws by which animals pass into one another.

And so the world received animals, mortal and immortal, and was fulfilled with them, and became a visible God, comprehending the visible, made in the image of the Intellectual, being the one perfect only-begotten heaven.

Section 2.

Nature in the aspect which she presented to a Greek philosopher of the fourth century before Christ is not easily reproduced to modern eyes. The associations of mythology and poetry have to be added, and the unconscious influence of science has to be subtracted, before we can behold the heavens or the earth as they appeared to the Greek. The philosopher himself was a child and also a man — a child in the range of his attainments, but also a great intelligence having an insight into nature, and often anticipations of the truth. He was full of original thoughts, and yet liable to be imposed upon by the most obvious fallacies. He occasionally confused numbers with ideas, and atoms with numbers; his a priori notions were out of all proportion to his experience. He was ready to explain the phenomena of the heavens by the most trivial analogies of earth. The experiments which nature worked for him he sometimes accepted, but he never tried experiments for himself which would either prove or disprove his theories. His knowledge was unequal; while in some branches, such as medicine and astronomy, he had made considerable proficiency, there were others, such as chemistry, electricity, mechanics, of which the very names were unknown to him. He was the natural enemy of mythology, and yet mythological ideas still retained their hold over him. He was endeavouring to form a conception of principles, but these principles or ideas were regarded by him as real powers or entities, to which the world had been subjected. He was always tending to argue from what was near to what was remote, from what was known to what was unknown, from man to the universe, and back again from the universe to man. While he was arranging the world, he was arranging the forms of thought in his own mind; and the light from within and the light from without often crossed and helped to confuse one another. He might be compared to a builder engaged in some great design, who could only dig with his hands because he was unprovided with common tools; or to some poet or musician, like Tynnichus (Ion), obliged to accommodate his lyric raptures to the limits of the tetrachord or of the flute.

The Hesiodic and Orphic cosmogonies were a phase of thought intermediate between mythology and philosophy and had a great influence on the beginnings of knowledge. There was nothing behind them; they were to physical science what the poems of Homer were to early Greek history. They made men think of the world as a whole; they carried the mind back into the infinity of past time; they suggested the first observation of the effects of fire and water on the earth's surface. To the ancient physics they stood much in the same relation which geology does to modern science. But the Greek was not, like the enquirer of the last generation, confined to a period of six thousand years; he was able to speculate freely on the effects of infinite ages in the production of physical phenomena. He could imagine cities which had existed time out of mind (States.; Laws), laws or forms of art and music which had lasted, 'not in word only, but in very truth, for ten thousand years' (Laws); he was aware that natural phenomena like the Delta of the Nile might have slowly accumulated in long periods of time (Hdt.). But he seems to have supposed that the course of events was recurring rather than progressive. To this he was probably led by the fixedness of Egyptian customs and the general observation that there were other civilisations in the world more ancient than that of Hellas.

The ancient philosophers found in mythology many ideas which, if not originally derived from nature, were easily transferred to her — such, for example, as love or hate, corresponding to attraction or repulsion; or the conception of necessity allied both to the regularity and irregularity of nature; or of chance, the nameless or unknown cause; or of justice, symbolizing the law of compensation; are of the Fates and Furies, typifying the fixed order or the extraordinary convulsions of nature. Their own interpretations of Homer and the poets were supposed by them to be the original meaning. Musing in themselves on the phenomena of nature, they were relieved at being able to utter the thoughts of their hearts in figures of speech which to them were not figures, and were already consecrated by tradition. Hesiod and the Orphic poets moved in a region of half-personification in which the meaning or principle appeared through the person. In their vaster conceptions of Chaos, Erebus, Aether, Night, and the like, the first rude attempts at generalization are dimly seen. The Gods themselves, especially the greater Gods, such as Zeus, Poseidon, Apollo, Athene, are universals as well as individuals. They were gradually becoming lost in a common conception of mind or God. They continued to exist for the purposes of ritual or of art; but from the sixth century onwards or even earlier there arose and gained strength in the minds of men the notion of 'one God, greatest among Gods and men, who was all sight, all hearing, all knowing' (Xenophanes).

Under the influence of such ideas, perhaps also deriving from the traditions of their own or of other nations scraps of medicine and astronomy, men came to the observation of nature. The Greek philosopher looked at the blue circle of the heavens and it flashed upon him that all things were one; the tumult of sense abated, and the mind found repose in the thought which former generations had been striving to realize. The first expression of this was some element, rarefied by degrees into a pure abstraction, and purged from any tincture of sense. Soon an inner world of ideas began to be unfolded, more absorbing, more overpowering, more abiding than the brightest of visible objects, which to the eye of the philosopher looking inward, seemed to pale before them, retaining only a faint and precarious existence. At the same time, the minds of men parted into the two great divisions of those who saw only a principle of motion, and of those who saw only a principle of rest, in nature and in themselves; there were born Heracliteans or Eleatics, as there have been in later ages born Aristotelians or Platonists. Like some philosophers in modern times, who are accused of making a theory first and finding their facts afterwards, the advocates of either opinion never thought of applying either to themselves or to their adversaries the criterion of fact. They were mastered by their ideas and not masters of them. Like the Heraclitean fanatics whom Plato has ridiculed in the Theaetetus, they were incapable of giving a reason of the faith that was in them, and had all the animosities of a religious sect. Yet, doubtless, there was some first impression derived from external nature, which, as in mythology, so also in philosophy, worked upon the minds of the first thinkers. Though incapable of induction or generalization in the modern sense, they caught an inspiration from the external world. The most general facts or appearances of nature, the circle of the universe, the nutritive power of water, the air which is the breath of life, the destructive force of fire, the seeming regularity of the greater part of nature and the irregularity of a remnant, the recurrence of day and night and of the seasons, the solid earth and the impalpable aether, were always present to them.

The great source of error and also the beginning of truth to them was reasoning from analogy; they could see resemblances, but not differences; and they were incapable of distinguishing illustration from argument. Analogy in modern times only points the way, and is immediately verified by experiment. The dreams and visions, which pass through the philosopher's mind, of resemblances between different classes of substances, or between the animal and vegetable world, are put into the refiner's fire, and the dross and other elements which adhere to them are purged away. But the contemporary of Plato and Socrates was incapable of resisting the power of any analogy which occurred to him, and was drawn into any consequences which seemed to follow. He had no methods of difference or of concomitant variations, by the use of which he could distinguish the accidental from the essential. He could not isolate phenomena, and he was helpless against the influence of any word which had an equivocal or double sense.

Yet without this crude use of analogy the ancient physical philosopher would have stood still; he could not have made even 'one guess among many' without comparison. The course of natural phenomena would have passed unheeded before his eyes, like fair sights or musical sounds before the eyes and ears of an animal. Even the fetichism of the savage is the beginning of reasoning; the assumption of the most fanciful of causes indicates a higher mental state than the absence of all enquiry about them. The tendency to argue from the higher to the lower, from man to the world, has led to many errors, but has also had an elevating influence on philosophy. The conception of the world as a whole, a person, an animal, has been the source of hasty generalizations; yet this general grasp of nature led also to a spirit of comprehensiveness in early philosophy, which has not increased, but rather diminished, as the fields of knowledge have become more divided. The modern physicist confines himself to one or perhaps two branches of science. But he comparatively seldom rises above his own department, and often falls under the narrowing influence which any single branch, when pursued to the exclusion of every other, has over the mind. Language, two, exercised a spell over the beginnings of physical philosophy, leading to error and sometimes to truth; for many thoughts were suggested by the double meanings of words (Greek), and the accidental distinctions of words sometimes led the ancient philosopher to make corresponding differences in things (Greek). 'If they are the same, why have they different names; or if they are different, why have they the same name?'— is an argument not easily answered in the infancy of knowledge. The modern philosopher has always been taught the lesson which he still imperfectly learns, that he must disengage himself from the influence of words. Nor are there wanting in Plato, who was himself too often the victim of them, impressive admonitions that we should regard not words but things (States.). But upon the whole, the ancients, though not entirely dominated by them, were much more subject to the influence of words than the moderns. They had no clear divisions of colours or substances; even the four elements were undefined; the fields of knowledge were not parted off. They were bringing order out of disorder, having a small grain of experience mingled in a confused heap of a priori notions. And yet, probably, their first impressions, the illusions and mirages of their fancy, created a greater intellectual activity and made a nearer approach to the truth than any patient investigation of isolated facts, for which the time had not yet come, could have accomplished.

There was one more illusion to which the ancient philosophers were subject, and against which Plato in his later dialogues seems to be struggling — the tendency to mere abstractions; not perceiving that pure abstraction is only negation, they thought that the greater the abstraction the greater the truth. Behind any pair of ideas a new idea which comprehended them — the (Greek), as it was technically termed — began at once to appear. Two are truer than three, one than two. The words 'being,' or 'unity,' or essence,' or 'good,' became sacred to them. They did not see that they had a word only, and in one sense the most unmeaning of words. They did not understand that the content of notions is in inverse proportion to their universality — the element which is the most widely diffused is also the thinnest; or, in the language of the common logic, the greater the extension the less the comprehension. But this vacant idea of a whole without parts, of a subject without predicates, a rest without motion, has been also the most fruitful of all ideas. It is the beginning of a priori thought, and indeed of thinking at all. Men were led to conceive it, not by a love of hasty generalization, but by a divine instinct, a dialectical enthusiasm, in which the human faculties seemed to yearn for enlargement. We know that 'being' is only the verb of existence, the copula, the most general symbol of relation, the first and most meagre of abstractions; but to some of the ancient philosophers this little word appeared to attain divine proportions, and to comprehend all truth. Being or essence, and similar words, represented to them a supreme or divine being, in which they thought that they found the containing and continuing principle of the universe. In a few years the human mind was peopled with abstractions; a new world was called into existence to give law and order to the old. But between them there was still a gulf, and no one could pass from the one to the other.

Number and figure were the greatest instruments of thought which were possessed by the Greek philosopher; having the same power over the mind which was exerted by abstract ideas, they were also capable of practical application. Many curious and, to the early thinker, mysterious properties of them came to light when they were compared with one another. They admitted of infinite multiplication and construction; in Pythagorean triangles or in proportions of 1:2:4:8 and 1:3:9:27, or compounds of them, the laws of the world seemed to be more than half revealed. They were also capable of infinite subdivision — a wonder and also a puzzle to the ancient thinker (Rep.). They were not, like being or essence, mere vacant abstractions, but admitted of progress and growth, while at the same time they confirmed a higher sentiment of the mind, that there was order in the universe. And so there began to be a real sympathy between the world within and the world without. The numbers and figures which were present to the mind's eye became visible to the eye of sense; the truth of nature was mathematics; the other properties of objects seemed to reappear only in the light of number. Law and morality also found a natural expression in number and figure. Instruments of such power and elasticity could not fail to be 'a most gracious assistance' to the first efforts of human intelligence.

There was another reason why numbers had so great an influence over the minds of early thinkers — they were verified by experience. Every use of them, even the most trivial, assured men of their truth; they were everywhere to be found, in the least things and the greatest alike. One, two, three, counted on the fingers was a 'trivial matter (Rep.), a little instrument out of which to create a world; but from these and by the help of these all our knowledge of nature has been developed. They were the measure of all things, and seemed to give law to all things; nature was rescued from chaos and confusion by their power; the notes of music, the motions of the stars, the forms of atoms, the evolution and recurrence of days, months, years, the military divisions of an army, the civil divisions of a state, seemed to afford a 'present witness' of them — what would have become of man or of the world if deprived of number (Rep.)? The mystery of number and the mystery of music were akin. There was a music of rhythm and of harmonious motion everywhere; and to the real connexion which existed between music and number, a fanciful or imaginary relation was superadded. There was a music of the spheres as well as of the notes of the lyre. If in all things seen there was number and figure, why should they not also pervade the unseen world, with which by their wonderful and unchangeable nature they seemed to hold communion?

Two other points strike us in the use which the ancient philosophers made of numbers. First, they applied to external nature the relations of them which they found in their own minds; and where nature seemed to be at variance with number, as for example in the case of fractions, they protested against her (Rep.; Arist. Metaph.). Having long meditated on the properties of 1:2:4:8, or 1:3:9:27, or of 3, 4, 5, they discovered in them many curious correspondences and were disposed to find in them the secret of the universe. Secondly, they applied number and figure equally to those parts of physics, such as astronomy or mechanics, in which the modern philosopher expects to find them, and to those in which he would never think of looking for them, such as physiology and psychology. For the sciences were not yet divided, and there was nothing really irrational in arguing that the same laws which regulated the heavenly bodies were partially applied to the erring limbs or brain of man. Astrology was the form which the lively fancy of ancient thinkers almost necessarily gave to astronomy. The observation that the lower principle, e.g. mechanics, is always seen in the higher, e.g. in the phenomena of life, further tended to perplex them. Plato's doctrine of the same and the other ruling the courses of the heavens and of the human body is not a mere vagary, but is a natural result of the state of knowledge and thought at which he had arrived.

When in modern times we contemplate the heavens, a certain amount of scientific truth imperceptibly blends, even with the cursory glance of an unscientific person. He knows that the earth is revolving round the sun, and not the sun around the earth. He does not imagine the earth to be the centre of the universe, and he has some conception of chemistry and the cognate sciences. A very different aspect of nature would have been present to the mind of the early Greek philosopher. He would have beheld the earth a surface only, not mirrored, however faintly, in the glass of science, but indissolubly connected with some theory of one, two, or more elements. He would have seen the world pervaded by number and figure, animated by a principle of motion, immanent in a principle of rest. He would have tried to construct the universe on a quantitative principle, seeming to find in endless combinations of geometrical figures or in the infinite variety of their sizes a sufficient account of the multiplicity of phenomena. To these a priori speculations he would add a rude conception of matter and his own immediate experience of health and disease. His cosmos would necessarily be imperfect and unequal, being the first attempt to impress form and order on the primaeval chaos of human knowledge. He would see all things as in a dream.

The ancient physical philosophers have been charged by Dr. Whewell and others with wasting their fine intelligences in wrong methods of enquiry; and their progress in moral and political philosophy has been sometimes contrasted with their supposed failure in physical investigations. 'They had plenty of ideas,' says Dr. Whewell, 'and plenty of facts; but their ideas did not accurately represent the facts with which they were acquainted.' This is a very crude and misleading way of describing ancient science. It is the mistake of an uneducated person — uneducated, that is, in the higher sense of the word — who imagines every one else to be like himself and explains every other age by his own. No doubt the ancients often fell into strange and fanciful errors: the time had not yet arrived for the slower and surer path of the modern inductive philosophy. But it remains to be shown that they could have done more in their age and country; or that the contributions which they made to the sciences with which they were acquainted are not as great upon the whole as those made by their successors. There is no single step in astronomy as great as that of the nameless Pythagorean who first conceived the world to be a body moving round the sun in space: there is no truer or more comprehensive principle than the application of mathematics alike to the heavenly bodies, and to the particles of matter. The ancients had not the instruments which would have enabled them to correct or verify their anticipations, and their opportunities of observation were limited. Plato probably did more for physical science by asserting the supremacy of mathematics than Aristotle or his disciples by their collections of facts. When the thinkers of modern times, following Bacon, undervalue or disparage the speculations of ancient philosophers, they seem wholly to forget the conditions of the world and of the human mind, under which they carried on their investigations. When we accuse them of being under the influence of words, do we suppose that we are altogether free from this illusion? When we remark that Greek physics soon became stationary or extinct, may we not observe also that there have been and may be again periods in the history of modern philosophy which have been barren and unproductive? We might as well maintain that Greek art was not real or great, because it had nihil simile aut secundum, as say that Greek physics were a failure because they admire no subsequent progress.

The charge of premature generalization which is often urged against ancient philosophers is really an anachronism. For they can hardly be said to have generalized at all. They may be said more truly to have cleared up and defined by the help of experience ideas which they already possessed. The beginnings of thought about nature must always have this character. A true method is the result of many ages of experiment and observation, and is ever going on and enlarging with the progress of science and knowledge. At first men personify nature, then they form impressions of nature, at last they conceive 'measure' or laws of nature. They pass out of mythology into philosophy. Early science is not a process of discovery in the modern sense; but rather a process of correcting by observation, and to a certain extent only, the first impressions of nature, which mankind, when they began to think, had received from poetry or language or unintelligent sense. Of all scientific truths the greatest and simplest is the uniformity of nature; this was expressed by the ancients in many ways, as fate, or necessity, or measure, or limit. Unexpected events, of which the cause was unknown to them, they attributed to chance (Thucyd.). But their conception of nature was never that of law interrupted by exceptions — a somewhat unfortunate metaphysical invention of modern times, which is at variance with facts and has failed to satisfy the requirements of thought.

Section 3.

Plato's account of the soul is partly mythical or figurative, and partly literal. Not that either he or we can draw a line between them, or say, 'This is poetry, this is philosophy'; for the transition from the one to the other is imperceptible. Neither must we expect to find in him absolute consistency. He is apt to pass from one level or stage of thought to another without always making it apparent that he is changing his ground. In such passages we have to interpret his meaning by the general spirit of his writings. To reconcile his inconsistencies would be contrary to the first principles of criticism and fatal to any true understanding of him.

There is a further difficulty in explaining this part of the Timaeus — the natural order of thought is inverted. We begin with the most abstract, and proceed from the abstract to the concrete. We are searching into things which are upon the utmost limit of human intelligence, and then of a sudden we fall rather heavily to the earth. There are no intermediate steps which lead from one to the other. But the abstract is a vacant form to us until brought into relation with man and nature. God and the world are mere names, like the Being of the Eleatics, unless some human qualities are added on to them. Yet the negation has a kind of unknown meaning to us. The priority of God and of the world, which he is imagined to have created, to all other existences, gives a solemn awe to them. And as in other systems of theology and philosophy, that of which we know least has the greatest interest to us.

There is no use in attempting to define or explain the first God in the Platonic system, who has sometimes been thought to answer to God the Father; or the world, in whom the Fathers of the Church seemed to recognize 'the firstborn of every creature.' Nor need we discuss at length how far Plato agrees in the later Jewish idea of creation, according to which God made the world out of nothing. For his original conception of matter as something which has no qualities is really a negation. Moreover in the Hebrew Scriptures the creation of the world is described, even more explicitly than in the Timaeus, not as a single act, but as a work or process which occupied six days. There is a chaos in both, and it would be untrue to say that the Greek, any more than the Hebrew, had any definite belief in the eternal existence of matter. The beginning of things vanished into the distance. The real creation began, not with matter, but with ideas. According to Plato in the Timaeus, God took of the same and the other, of the divided and undivided, of the finite and infinite, and made essence, and out of the three combined created the soul of the world. To the soul he added a body formed out of the four elements. The general meaning of these words is that God imparted determinations of thought, or, as we might say, gave law and variety to the material universe. The elements are moving in a disorderly manner before the work of creation begins; and there is an eternal pattern of the world, which, like the 'idea of good,' is not the Creator himself, but not separable from him. The pattern too, though eternal, is a creation, a world of thought prior to the world of sense, which may be compared to the wisdom of God in the book of Ecclesiasticus, or to the 'God in the form of a globe' of the old Eleatic philosophers. The visible, which already exists, is fashioned in the likeness of this eternal pattern. On the other hand, there is no truth of which Plato is more firmly convinced than of the priority of the soul to the body, both in the universe and in man. So inconsistent are the forms in which he describes the works which no tongue can utter — his language, as he himself says, partaking of his own uncertainty about the things of which he is speaking.

We may remark in passing, that the Platonic compared with the Jewish description of the process of creation has less of freedom or spontaneity. The Creator in Plato is still subject to a remnant of necessity which he cannot wholly overcome. When his work is accomplished he remains in his own nature. Plato is more sensible than the Hebrew prophet of the existence of evil, which he seeks to put as far as possible out of the way of God. And he can only suppose this to be accomplished by God retiring into himself and committing the lesser works of creation to inferior powers. (Compare, however, Laws for another solution of the difficulty.)

Nor can we attach any intelligible meaning to his words when he speaks of the visible being in the image of the invisible. For how can that which is divided be like that which is undivided? Or that which is changing be the copy of that which is unchanging? All the old difficulties about the ideas come back upon us in an altered form. We can imagine two worlds, one of which is the mere double of the other, or one of which is an imperfect copy of the other, or one of which is the vanishing ideal of the other; but we cannot imagine an intellectual world which has no qualities —'a thing in itself'— a point which has no parts or magnitude, which is nowhere, and nothing. This cannot be the archetype according to which God made the world, and is in reality, whether in Plato or in Kant, a mere negative residuum of human thought.

There is another aspect of the same difficulty which appears to have no satisfactory solution. In what relation does the archetype stand to the Creator himself? For the idea or pattern of the world is not the thought of God, but a separate, self-existent nature, of which creation is the copy. We can only reply, (1) that to the mind of Plato subject and object were not yet distinguished; (2) that he supposes the process of creation to take place in accordance with his own theory of ideas; and as we cannot give a consistent account of the one, neither can we of the other. He means (3) to say that the creation of the world is not a material process of working with legs and arms, but ideal and intellectual; according to his own fine expression, 'the thought of God made the God that was to be.' He means (4) to draw an absolute distinction between the invisible or unchangeable which is or is the place of mind or being, and the world of sense or becoming which is visible and changing. He means (5) that the idea of the world is prior to the world, just as the other ideas are prior to sensible objects; and like them may be regarded as eternal and self-existent, and also, like the IDEA of good, may be viewed apart from the divine mind.

There are several other questions which we might ask and which can receive no answer, or at least only an answer of the same kind as the preceding. How can matter be conceived to exist without form? Or, how can the essences or forms of things be distinguished from the eternal ideas, or essence itself from the soul? Or, how could there have been motion in the chaos when as yet time was not? Or, how did chaos come into existence, if not by the will of the Creator? Or, how could there have been a time when the world was not, if time was not? Or, how could the Creator have taken portions of an indivisible same? Or, how could space or anything else have been eternal when time is only created? Or, how could the surfaces of geometrical figures have formed solids? We must reply again that we cannot follow Plato in all his inconsistencies, but that the gaps of thought are probably more apparent to us than to him. He would, perhaps, have said that 'the first things are known only to God and to him of men whom God loves.' How often have the gaps in Theology been concealed from the eye of faith! And we may say that only by an effort of metaphysical imagination can we hope to understand Plato from his own point of view; we must not ask for consistency. Everywhere we find traces of the Platonic theory of knowledge expressed in an objective form, which by us has to be translated into the subjective, before we can attach any meaning to it. And this theory is exhibited in so many different points of view, that we cannot with any certainty interpret one dialogue by another; e.g. the Timaeus by the Parmenides or Phaedrus or Philebus.

The soul of the world may also be conceived as the personification of the numbers and figures in which the heavenly bodies move. Imagine these as in a Pythagorean dream, stripped of qualitative difference and reduced to mathematical abstractions. They too conform to the principle of the same, and may be compared with the modern conception of laws of nature. They are in space, but not in time, and they are the makers of time. They are represented as constantly thinking of the same; for thought in the view of Plato is equivalent to truth or law, and need not imply a human consciousness, a conception which is familiar enough to us, but has no place, hardly even a name, in ancient Greek philosophy. To this principle of the same is opposed the principle of the other — the principle of irregularity and disorder, of necessity and chance, which is only partially impressed by mathematical laws and figures. (We may observe by the way, that the principle of the other, which is the principle of plurality and variation in the Timaeus, has nothing in common with the 'other' of the Sophist, which is the principle of determination.)

The element of the same dominates to a certain extent over the other — the fixed stars keep the 'wanderers' of the inner circle in their courses, and a similar principle of fixedness or order appears to regulate the bodily constitution of man. But there still remains a rebellious seed of evil derived from the original chaos, which is the source of disorder in the world, and of vice and disease in man.

But what did Plato mean by essence, (Greek), which is the intermediate nature compounded of the Same and the Other, and out of which, together with these two, the soul of the world is created? It is difficult to explain a process of thought so strange and unaccustomed to us, in which modern distinctions run into one another and are lost sight of. First, let us consider once more the meaning of the Same and the Other. The Same is the unchanging and indivisible, the heaven of the fixed stars, partaking of the divine nature, which, having law in itself, gives law to all besides and is the element of order and permanence in man and on the earth. It is the rational principle, mind regarded as a work, as creation — not as the creator. The old tradition of Parmenides and of the Eleatic Being, the foundation of so much in the philosophy of Greece and of the world, was lingering in Plato's mind. The Other is the variable or changing element, the residuum of disorder or chaos, which cannot be reduced to order, nor altogether banished, the source of evil, seen in the errors of man and also in the wanderings of the planets, a necessity which protrudes through nature. Of this too there was a shadow in the Eleatic philosophy in the realm of opinion, which, like a mist, seemed to darken the purity of truth in itself. — So far the words of Plato may perhaps find an intelligible meaning. But when he goes on to speak of the Essence which is compounded out of both, the track becomes fainter and we can only follow him with hesitating steps. But still we find a trace reappearing of the teaching of Anaxagoras: 'All was confusion, and then mind came and arranged things.' We have already remarked that Plato was not acquainted with the modern distinction of subject and object, and therefore he sometimes confuses mind and the things of mind —(Greek) and (Greek). By (Greek) he clearly means some conception of the intelligible and the intelligent; it belongs to the class of (Greek). Matter, being, the Same, the eternal — for any of these terms, being almost vacant of meaning, is equally suitable to express indefinite existence — are compared or united with the Other or Diverse, and out of the union or comparison is elicited the idea of intelligence, the 'One in many,' brighter than any Promethean fire (Phil.), which co-existing with them and so forming a new existence, is or becomes the intelligible world . . . So we may perhaps venture to paraphrase or interpret or put into other words the parable in which Plato has wrapped up his conception of the creation of the world. The explanation may help to fill up with figures of speech the void of knowledge.

The entire compound was divided by the Creator in certain proportions and reunited; it was then cut into two strips, which were bent into an inner circle and an outer, both moving with an uniform motion around a centre, the outer circle containing the fixed, the inner the wandering stars. The soul of the world was diffused everywhere from the centre to the circumference. To this God gave a body, consisting at first of fire and earth, and afterwards receiving an addition of air and water; because solid bodies, like the world, are always connected by two middle terms and not by one. The world was made in the form of a globe, and all the material elements were exhausted in the work of creation.

The proportions in which the soul of the world as well as the human soul is divided answer to a series of numbers 1, 2, 3, 4, 9, 8, 27, composed of the two Pythagorean progressions 1, 2, 4, 8 and 1, 3, 9, 27, of which the number 1 represents a point, 2 and 3 lines, 4 and 8, 9 and 27 the squares and cubes respectively of 2 and 3. This series, of which the intervals are afterwards filled up, probably represents (1) the diatonic scale according to the Pythagoreans and Plato; (2) the order and distances of the heavenly bodies; and (3) may possibly contain an allusion to the music of the spheres, which is referred to in the myth at the end of the Republic. The meaning of the words that 'solid bodies are always connected by two middle terms' or mean proportionals has been much disputed. The most received explanation is that of Martin, who supposes that Plato is only speaking of surfaces and solids compounded of prime numbers (i.e. of numbers not made up of two factors, or, in other words, only measurable by unity). The square of any such number represents a surface, the cube a solid. The squares of any two such numbers (e.g. 2 squared, 3 squared = 4, 9), have always a single mean proportional (e.g. 4 and 9 have the single mean 6), whereas the cubes of primes (e.g. 3 cubed and 5 cubed) have always two mean proportionals (e.g. 27:45:75:125). But to this explanation of Martin's it may be objected, (1) that Plato nowhere says that his proportion is to be limited to prime numbers; (2) that the limitation of surfaces to squares is also not to be found in his words; nor (3) is there any evidence to show that the distinction of prime from other numbers was known to him. What Plato chiefly intends to express is that a solid requires a stronger bond than a surface; and that the double bond which is given by two means is stronger than the single bond given by one. Having reflected on the singular numerical phenomena of the existence of one mean proportional between two square numbers are rather perhaps only between the two lowest squares; and of two mean proportionals between two cubes, perhaps again confining his attention to the two lowest cubes, he finds in the latter symbol an expression of the relation of the elements, as in the former an image of the combination of two surfaces. Between fire and earth, the two extremes, he remarks that there are introduced, not one, but two elements, air and water, which are compared to the two mean proportionals between two cube numbers. The vagueness of his language does not allow us to determine whether anything more than this was intended by him.

Leaving the further explanation of details, which the reader will find discussed at length in Boeckh and Martin, we may now return to the main argument: Why did God make the world? Like man, he must have a purpose; and his purpose is the diffusion of that goodness or good which he himself is. The term 'goodness' is not to be understood in this passage as meaning benevolence or love, in the Christian sense of the term, but rather law, order, harmony, like the idea of good in the Republic. The ancient mythologers, and even the Hebrew prophets, had spoken of the jealousy of God; and the Greek had imagined that there was a Nemesis always attending the prosperity of mortals. But Plato delights to think of God as the author of order in his works, who, like a father, lives over again in his children, and can never have too much of good or friendship among his creatures. Only, as there is a certain remnant of evil inherent in matter which he cannot get rid of, he detaches himself from them and leaves them to themselves, that he may be guiltless of their faults and sufferings.

Between the ideal and the sensible Plato interposes the two natures of time and space. Time is conceived by him to be only the shadow or image of eternity which ever is and never has been or will be, but is described in a figure only as past or future. This is one of the great thoughts of early philosophy, which are still as difficult to our minds as they were to the early thinkers; or perhaps more difficult, because we more distinctly see the consequences which are involved in such an hypothesis. All the objections which may be urged against Kant's doctrine of the ideality of space and time at once press upon us. If time is unreal, then all which is contained in time is unreal — the succession of human thoughts as well as the flux of sensations; there is no connecting link between (Greek) and (Greek). Yet, on the other hand, we are conscious that knowledge is independent of time, that truth is not a thing of yesterday or tomorrow, but an 'eternal now.' To the 'spectator of all time and all existence' the universe remains at rest. The truths of geometry and arithmetic in all their combinations are always the same. The generations of men, like the leaves of the forest, come and go, but the mathematical laws by which the world is governed remain, and seem as if they could never change. The ever-present image of space is transferred to time — succession is conceived as extension. (We remark that Plato does away with the above and below in space, as he has done away with the absolute existence of past and future.) The course of time, unless regularly marked by divisions of number, partakes of the indefiniteness of the Heraclitean flux. By such reflections we may conceive the Greek to have attained the metaphysical conception of eternity, which to the Hebrew was gained by meditation on the Divine Being. No one saw that this objective was really a subjective, and involved the subjectivity of all knowledge. 'Non in tempore sed cum tempore finxit Deus mundum,' says St. Augustine, repeating a thought derived from the Timaeus, but apparently unconscious of the results to which his doctrine would have led.

The contradictions involved in the conception of time or motion, like the infinitesimal in space, were a source of perplexity to the mind of the Greek, who was driven to find a point of view above or beyond them. They had sprung up in the decline of the Eleatic philosophy and were very familiar to Plato, as we gather from the Parmenides. The consciousness of them had led the great Eleatic philosopher to describe the nature of God or Being under negatives. He sings of 'Being unbegotten and imperishable, unmoved and never-ending, which never was nor will be, but always is, one and continuous, which cannot spring from any other; for it cannot be said or imagined not to be.' The idea of eternity was for a great part a negation. There are regions of speculation in which the negative is hardly separable from the positive, and even seems to pass into it. Not only Buddhism, but Greek as well as Christian philosophy, show that it is quite possible that the human mind should retain an enthusiasm for mere negations. In different ages and countries there have been forms of light in which nothing could be discerned and which have nevertheless exercised a life-giving and illumining power. For the higher intelligence of man seems to require, not only something above sense, but above knowledge, which can only be described as Mind or Being or Truth or God or the unchangeable and eternal element, in the expression of which all predicates fail and fall short. Eternity or the eternal is not merely the unlimited in time but the truest of all Being, the most real of all realities, the most certain of all knowledge, which we nevertheless only see through a glass darkly. The passionate earnestness of Parmenides contrasts with the vacuity of the thought which he is revolving in his mind.

Space is said by Plato to be the 'containing vessel or nurse of generation.' Reflecting on the simplest kinds of external objects, which to the ancients were the four elements, he was led to a more general notion of a substance, more or less like themselves, out of which they were fashioned. He would not have them too precisely distinguished. Thus seems to have arisen the first dim perception of (Greek) or matter, which has played so great a part in the metaphysical philosophy of Aristotle and his followers. But besides the material out of which the elements are made, there is also a space in which they are contained. There arises thus a second nature which the senses are incapable of discerning and which can hardly be referred to the intelligible class. For it is and it is not, it is nowhere when filled, it is nothing when empty. Hence it is said to be discerned by a kind of spurious or analogous reason, partaking so feebly of existence as to be hardly perceivable, yet always reappearing as the containing mother or nurse of all things. It had not that sort of consistency to Plato which has been given to it in modern times by geometry and metaphysics. Neither of the Greek words by which it is described are so purely abstract as the English word 'space' or the Latin 'spatium.' Neither Plato nor any other Greek would have spoken of (Greek) or (Greek) in the same manner as we speak of 'time' and 'space.'

Yet space is also of a very permanent or even eternal nature; and Plato seems more willing to admit of the unreality of time than of the unreality of space; because, as he says, all things must necessarily exist in space. We, on the other hand, are disposed to fancy that even if space were annihilated time might still survive. He admits indeed that our knowledge of space is of a dreamy kind, and is given by a spurious reason without the help of sense. (Compare the hypotheses and images of Rep.) It is true that it does not attain to the clearness of ideas. But like them it seems to remain, even if all the objects contained in it are supposed to have vanished away. Hence it was natural for Plato to conceive of it as eternal. We must remember further that in his attempt to realize either space or matter the two abstract ideas of weight and extension, which are familiar to us, had never passed before his mind.

Thus far God, working according to an eternal pattern, out of his goodness has created the same, the other, and the essence (compare the three principles of the Philebus — the finite, the infinite, and the union of the two), and out of them has formed the outer circle of the fixed stars and the inner circle of the planets, divided according to certain musical intervals; he has also created time, the moving image of eternity, and space, existing by a sort of necessity and hardly distinguishable from matter. The matter out of which the world is formed is not absolutely void, but retains in the chaos certain germs or traces of the elements. These Plato, like Empedocles, supposed to be four in number — fire, air, earth, and water. They were at first mixed together; but already in the chaos, before God fashioned them by form and number, the greater masses of the elements had an appointed place. Into the confusion (Greek) which preceded Plato does not attempt further to penetrate. They are called elements, but they are so far from being elements (Greek) or letters in the higher sense that they are not even syllables or first compounds. The real elements are two triangles, the rectangular isosceles which has but one form, and the most beautiful of the many forms of scalene, which is half of an equilateral triangle. By the combination of these triangles which exist in an infinite variety of sizes, the surfaces of the four elements are constructed.

That there were only five regular solids was already known to the ancients, and out of the surfaces which he has formed Plato proceeds to generate the four first of the five. He perhaps forgets that he is only putting together surfaces and has not provided for their transformation into solids. The first solid is a regular pyramid, of which the base and sides are formed by four equilateral or twenty-four scalene triangles. Each of the four solid angles in this figure is a little larger than the largest of obtuse angles. The second solid is composed of the same triangles, which unite as eight equilateral triangles, and make one solid angle out of four plane angles — six of these angles form a regular octahedron. The third solid is a regular icosahedron, having twenty triangular equilateral bases, and therefore 120 rectangular scalene triangles. The fourth regular solid, or cube, is formed by the combination of four isosceles triangles into one square and of six squares into a cube. The fifth regular solid, or dodecahedron, cannot be formed by a combination of either of these triangles, but each of its faces may be regarded as composed of thirty triangles of another kind. Probably Plato notices this as the only remaining regular polyhedron, which from its approximation to a globe, and possibly because, as Plutarch remarks, it is composed of $12 \times 30 = 360$ scalene triangles (Platon. Quaest.), representing thus the signs and degrees of the Zodiac, as well as the months and days of the year, God may be said to have 'used in the delineation of the universe.' According to Plato earth was composed of cubes, fire of regular pyramids, air of regular octahedrons, water of regular icosahedrons. The stability of the last three increases with the number of their sides.

The elements are supposed to pass into one another, but we must remember that these transformations are not the transformations of real solids, but of imaginary geometrical figures; in other words, we are composing and decomposing the faces of substances and not the substances themselves — it is a house of cards which we are pulling to pieces and putting together again (compare however Laws). Yet perhaps Plato may regard these sides or faces as only the forms which are impressed on pre-existent matter. It is remarkable that he should speak of each of these solids as a possible world in itself, though upon the whole he inclines to the opinion that they form one world and not five. To suppose that there is an infinite number of worlds, as Democritus (Hippolyt. Ref. Haer. I.) had said, would be, as he satirically observes, 'the characteristic of a very indefinite and ignorant mind.'

The twenty triangular faces of an icosahedron form the faces or sides of two regular octahedrons and of a regular pyramid ($20 = 8 \times 2 + 4$); and therefore, according to Plato, a particle of water when decomposed is supposed to give two particles of air and one of fire. So because an octahedron gives the sides of two pyramids ($8 = 4 \times 2$), a particle of air is resolved into two particles of fire.

The transformation is effected by the superior power or number of the conquering elements. The manner of the change is (1) a separation of portions of the elements from the masses in which they are collected; (2) a resolution of them into their original triangles; and (3) a reunion of them in new forms. Plato himself proposes the question, Why does motion continue at all when the elements are settled in their places? He answers that although the force of attraction is continually drawing similar elements to the same spot, still the revolution of the universe exercises a condensing power, and thrusts them again out of their natural places. Thus want of uniformity, the condition of motion, is produced. In all such disturbances of matter there is an alternative for the weaker element: it may escape to its kindred, or take the form of the stronger

— becoming denser, if it be denser, or rarer if rarer. This is true of fire, air, and water, which, being composed of similar triangles, are interchangeable; earth, however, which has triangles peculiar to itself, is capable of dissolution, but not of change. Of the interchangeable elements, fire, the rarest, can only become a denser, and water, the densest, only a rarer: but air may become a denser or a rarer. No single particle of the elements is visible, but only the aggregates of them are seen. The subordinate species depend, not upon differences of form in the original triangles, but upon differences of size. The obvious physical phenomena from which Plato has gathered his views of the relations of the elements seem to be the effect of fire upon air, water, and earth, and the effect of water upon earth. The particles are supposed by him to be in a perpetual process of circulation caused by inequality. This process of circulation does not admit of a vacuum, as he tells us in his strange account of respiration.

Of the phenomena of light and heavy he speaks afterwards, when treating of sensation, but they may be more conveniently considered by us in this place. They are not, he says, to be explained by 'above' and 'below,' which in the universal globe have no existence, but by the attraction of similars towards the great masses of similar substances; fire to fire, air to air, water to water, earth to earth. Plato's doctrine of attraction implies not only (1) the attraction of similar elements to one another, but also (2) of smaller bodies to larger ones. Had he confined himself to the latter he would have arrived, though, perhaps, without any further result or any sense of the greatness of the discovery, at the modern doctrine of gravitation. He does not observe that water has an equal tendency towards both water and earth. So easily did the most obvious facts which were inconsistent with his theories escape him.

The general physical doctrines of the Timaeus may be summed up as follows: (1) Plato supposes the greater masses of the elements to have been already settled in their places at the creation: (2) they are four in number, and are formed of rectangular triangles variously combined into regular solid figures: (3) three of them, fire, air, and water, admit of transformation into one another; the fourth, earth, cannot be similarly transformed: (4) different sizes of the same triangles form the lesser species of each element: (5) there is an attraction of like to like — smaller masses of the same kind being drawn towards greater: (6) there is no void, but the particles of matter are ever pushing one another round and round (Greek). Like the atomists, Plato attributes the differences between the elements to differences in geometrical figures. But he does not explain the process by which surfaces become solids; and he characteristically ridicules Democritus for not seeing that the worlds are finite and not infinite.

Section 4.

The astronomy of Plato is based on the two principles of the same and the other, which God combined in the creation of the world. The soul, which is compounded of the same, the other, and the essence, is diffused from the centre to the circumference of the heavens. We speak of a soul of the universe; but more truly regarded, the universe of the Timaeus is a soul, governed by mind, and holding in solution a residuum of matter or evil, which the author of the world is unable to expel, and of which Plato cannot tell us the origin. The creation, in Plato's sense, is really the creation of order; and the first step in giving order is the division of the heavens into an inner and outer circle of the other and the same, of the divisible and the indivisible, answering to the two spheres, of the planets and of the world beyond them, all together moving around the earth, which is their centre. To us there is a difficulty in apprehending how that which is at rest can also be in motion, or that which is indivisible exist in space. But the whole description is so ideal and imaginative, that we can hardly venture to attribute to many of Plato's words in the Timaeus any more meaning than to his mythical account of the heavens in the Republic and in the Phaedrus. (Compare his denial of the 'blasphemous opinion' that there are planets or wandering stars; all alike move in circles — Laws.) The stars are the habitations of the souls of men, from which they come and to which they return. In attributing to the fixed stars only the most perfect motion — that which is on the same spot or circulating around the same — he might perhaps have said that to 'the spectator of all time and all existence,' to borrow once more his own grand expression, or viewed, in the language of Spinoza, 'sub specie aeternitatis,' they were still at rest, but appeared to move in order to teach men the periods of time. Although absolutely in motion, they are relatively at rest; or we may conceive of them as resting, while the space in which they are contained, or the whole anima mundi, revolves.

The universe revolves around a centre once in twenty-four hours, but the orbits of the fixed stars take a different direction from those of the planets. The outer and the inner sphere cross one another and meet again at a point opposite to that of their first contact; the first moving in a circle from left to right along the side of a parallelogram which is supposed to be inscribed in it, the second also moving in a circle along the diagonal of the same parallelogram from right to left; or, in other words, the first describing the path of the equator, the second, the path of the ecliptic. The motion of the second is controlled by the first, and hence the oblique line in which the planets are supposed to move becomes a spiral. The motion of the same is said to be undivided, whereas the inner motion is split into seven unequal orbits — the intervals between them being in the ratio of two and three, three of either:— the Sun, moving in the opposite direction to Mercury and Venus, but with equal swiftness; the remaining four, Moon, Saturn, Mars, Jupiter, with unequal swiftness to the former three and to one another. Thus arises the following progression:— Moon 1, Sun 2, Venus 3, Mercury 4, Mars 8, Jupiter 9, Saturn 27. This series of numbers is the compound of the two Pythagorean ratios, having the same intervals, though not in the same order, as the mixture which was originally divided in forming the soul of the world.

Plato was struck by the phenomenon of Mercury, Venus, and the Sun appearing to overtake and be overtaken by one another. The true reason of this, namely, that they lie within the circle of the earth's orbit, was unknown to him, and the reason which he gives — that the two former move in an opposite direction to the latter — is far from explaining the appearance of them in the heavens. All the planets, including the sun, are carried round in the daily motion of the circle of the fixed stars, and they have a second or oblique motion which gives the explanation of the different lengths of the sun's course in different parts of the earth. The fixed stars have also two movements — a forward movement in their orbit which is common to the whole circle; and a movement on the same spot around an axis, which Plato calls the movement of thought about the same. In this latter respect they are more perfect than the wandering stars, as Plato himself terms them in the Timaeus, although in the Laws he condemns the appellation as blasphemous.

The revolution of the world around earth, which is accomplished in a single day and night, is described as being the most perfect or intelligent. Yet Plato also speaks of an 'annus magnus' or cyclical year, in which periods wonderful for their complexity are found to coincide in a perfect number, i.e. a number which equals the sum of its factors, as $6 = 1 + 2 + 3$. This, although not literally contradictory, is in spirit irreconcilable with the perfect revolution of twenty-four hours. The same remark may be applied to the complexity of the appearances and occultations of the stars, which, if the outer heaven is supposed to be moving around the centre once in twenty- four hours, must be confined to the effects produced by the seven planets. Plato seems to confuse the actual observation of the heavens with his desire to find in them mathematical perfection. The same spirit is carried yet further by him in the passage already quoted from the Laws, in which he affirms their wanderings to be an appearance only, which a little knowledge of mathematics would enable men to correct.

We have now to consider the much discussed question of the rotation or immobility of the earth. Plato's doctrine on this subject is contained in the following words:—'The earth, which is our nurse, compacted (OR revolving) around the pole which is extended through the universe, he made to be the guardian and artificer of night and day, first and eldest of gods that are in the interior of heaven'. There is an unfortunate doubt in this passage (1) about the meaning of the word (Greek), which is translated either 'compacted' or 'revolving,' and is equally capable of both explanations. A doubt (2) may also be raised as to whether the words 'artificer of day and night' are consistent with the mere passive causation of them, produced by the immobility of the earth in the midst of the circling universe. We must admit, further, (3) that Aristotle attributed to Plato the doctrine of the rotation of the earth on its axis. On the other hand it has been urged that if the earth goes round with the outer heaven and sun in twenty-four hours, there is no way of accounting for the alternation of day and night; since the equal motion of the earth and sun would have the effect of absolute immobility. To which it may be replied that Plato never says that the earth goes round with the outer heaven and sun; although the whole question depends on the relation of earth and sun, their movements are nowhere precisely described. But if we suppose, with Mr. Grote, that the diurnal rotation of the earth on its axis and the revolution of the sun and outer heaven precisely coincide, it would be difficult to imagine that Plato was unaware of the consequence. For though he was ignorant of many things which are familiar to us, and often confused in his ideas where we have become clear, we have no right to attribute to him a childish want of reasoning about very simple facts, or an inability to understand the necessary and obvious deductions from geometrical figures or movements. Of the causes of day and night the pre-Socratic philosophers, and especially the Pythagoreans, gave various accounts, and therefore the question can hardly be imagined to have escaped him. On the other hand it may be urged that the further step, however simple and obvious, is just what Plato often seems to be ignorant of, and that as there is no limit to his insight, there is also no limit to the blindness which sometimes obscures his intelligence (compare the construction of solids out of surfaces in his account of the creation of the world, or the attraction of similars to similars). Further, Mr. Grote supposes, not that (Greek) means 'revolving,' or that this is the sense in which Aristotle understood the word, but that the rotation of the earth is necessarily implied in its adherence to the cosmical axis. But (a) if, as Mr Grote assumes, Plato did not see that the rotation of the earth on its axis and of the sun and outer heavens around the earth in equal times was inconsistent with the alternation of day and night, neither need we suppose that he would have seen the immobility of the earth to be inconsistent with the rotation of the axis. And (b) what proof is there that the axis of the world revolves at all? (c) The comparison of the two passages quoted by Mr Grote (see his pamphlet on 'The Rotation of the Earth') from Aristotle De Coelo, Book II (Greek) clearly shows, although this is a matter of minor importance, that Aristotle, as Proclus and Simplicius supposed, understood (Greek) in the Timaeus to mean 'revolving.' For the second passage, in which motion on an axis is expressly mentioned, refers to the first, but this would be unmeaning unless (Greek) in the first passage meant rotation on an axis. (4) The immobility of the earth is more in accordance with Plato's other writings than the opposite hypothesis. For in the Phaedo the earth is described as the centre of the world, and is not said to be in motion. In the Republic the pilgrims appear to be looking out from the earth upon the motions of the heavenly bodies; in the Phaedrus, Hestia, who remains immovable in the house of Zeus while the other gods go in procession, is called the first and eldest of the gods, and is probably the symbol of the earth. The silence of Plato in these and in some other passages (Laws) in which he might be expected to speak of the rotation of the earth, is more favourable to the doctrine of its immobility than to the opposite. If he had meant to say that the earth revolves on its axis, he would have said so in distinct words, and have explained the relation of its movements to those of the other heavenly bodies. (5) The meaning of the words 'artificer of day and night' is literally true according to Plato's view. For the alternation of day and night is not produced by the motion of the heavens alone, or by the immobility of the earth alone, but by both together; and that which has the inherent force or energy to remain at rest when all other bodies are moving, may be truly said to act, equally with them. (6) We should not lay too much stress on Aristotle or the writer De Caelo having adopted the other interpretation of the words, although Alexander of Aphrodisias thinks that he could not have been ignorant either of the doctrine of Plato or of the sense which he intended to give to the word (Greek). For the citations of Plato in Aristotle are frequently misinterpreted by him; and he seems hardly ever to have had in his mind the connection in which they occur. In this instance the allusion is very slight, and there is no reason to suppose that the diurnal revolution of the heavens was present to his mind. Hence we need not attribute to him the error from which we are defending Plato.

After weighing one against the other all these complicated probabilities, the final conclusion at which we arrive is that there is nearly as much to be said on the one side of the question as on the other, and that we are not perfectly certain, whether, as Bockh and the majority of commentators, ancient as well as modern, are inclined to believe, Plato thought that the earth was at rest in the centre of the universe, or, as Aristotle and Mr. Grote suppose, that it revolved on its axis. Whether we assume the earth to be stationary in the centre of the universe, or to revolve with the heavens, no explanation is given of the variation in the length of days and nights at different times of the year. The relations of the earth and heavens are so indistinct in the Timaeus and so figurative in the Phaedo, Phaedrus and Republic, that we must give up the hope of ascertaining how they were imagined by Plato, if he had any fixed or scientific conception of them at all.

Section 5.

The soul of the world is framed on the analogy of the soul of man, and many traces of anthropomorphism blend with Plato's highest flights of idealism. The heavenly bodies are endowed with thought; the principles of the same and other exist in the universe as well as in the human mind. The soul of man is made out of the remains of the elements which had been used in creating the soul of the world; these remains, however, are diluted to the third degree; by this Plato expresses the measure of the difference between the soul human and divine. The human soul, like the cosmical, is framed before the body, as the mind is before the soul of either — this is the order of the divine work — and the finer parts of the body, which are more akin to the soul, such as the spinal marrow, are prior to the bones and flesh. The brain, the containing vessel of the divine part of the soul, is (nearly) in the form of a globe, which is the image of the gods, who are the stars, and of the universe.

There is, however, an inconsistency in Plato's manner of conceiving the soul of man; he cannot get rid of the element of necessity which is allowed to enter. He does not, like Kant, attempt to vindicate for men a freedom out of space and time; but he acknowledges him to be subject to the influence of external causes, and leaves hardly any place for freedom of the will. The lusts of men are caused by their bodily constitution, though they may be increased by bad education and bad laws, which implies that they may be decreased by good education and good laws. He appears to have an inkling of the truth that to the higher nature of man evil is involuntary. This is mixed up with the view which, while apparently agreeing with it, is in reality the opposite of it, that vice is due to physical causes. In the Timaeus, as well as in the Laws, he also regards vices and crimes as simply involuntary; they are diseases analogous to the diseases of the body, and arising out of the same causes. If we draw together the opposite poles of Plato's system, we find that, like Spinoza, he combines idealism with fatalism.

The soul of man is divided by him into three parts, answering roughly to the charioteer and steeds of the Phaedrus, and to the (Greek) of the Republic and Nicomachean Ethics. First, there is the immortal nature of which the brain is the seat, and which is akin to the soul of the universe. This alone thinks and knows and is the ruler of the whole. Secondly, there is the higher mortal soul which, though liable to perturbations of her own, takes the side of reason against the lower appetites. The seat of this is the heart, in which courage, anger, and all the nobler affections are supposed to reside. There the veins all meet; it is their centre or house of guard whence they carry the orders of the thinking being to the extremities of his kingdom. There is also a third or appetitive soul, which receives the commands of the immortal part, not immediately but mediately, through the liver, which reflects on its surface the admonitions and threats of the reason.

The liver is imagined by Plato to be a smooth and bright substance, having a store of sweetness and also of bitterness, which reason freely uses in the execution of her mandates. In this region, as ancient superstition told, were to be found intimations of the future. But Plato is careful to observe that although such knowledge is given to the inferior parts of man, it requires to be interpreted by the superior. Reason, and not enthusiasm, is the true guide of man; he is only inspired when he is demented by some distemper or possession. The ancient saying, that 'only a man in his senses can judge of his own actions,' is approved by modern philosophy too. The same irony which appears in Plato's remark, that 'the men of old time must surely have known the gods who were their ancestors, and we should believe them as custom requires,' is also manifest in his account of divination.

The appetitive soul is seated in the belly, and there imprisoned like a wild beast, far away from the council chamber, as Plato graphically calls the head, in order that the animal passions may not interfere with the deliberations of reason. Though the soul is said by him to be prior to the body, yet we cannot help seeing that it is constructed on the model of the body — the threefold division into the rational, passionate, and appetitive corresponding to the head, heart and belly. The human soul differs from the soul of the world in this respect, that it is enveloped and finds its expression in matter, whereas the soul of the world is not only enveloped or diffused in matter, but is the element in which matter moves. The breath of man is within him, but the air or aether of heaven is the element which surrounds him and all things.

Pleasure and pain are attributed in the Timaeus to the suddenness of our sensations — the first being a sudden restoration, the second a sudden violation, of nature (Phileb.). The sensations become conscious to us when they are exceptional. Sight is not attended either by pleasure or pain, but hunger and the appeasing of hunger are pleasant and painful because they are extraordinary.

Section 6.

I shall not attempt to connect the physiological speculations of Plato either with ancient or modern medicine. What light I can throw upon them will be derived from the comparison of them with his general system.

There is no principle so apparent in the physics of the Timaeus, or in ancient physics generally, as that of continuity. The world is conceived of as a whole, and the elements are formed into and out of one another; the varieties of substances and processes are hardly known or noticed. And in a similar manner the human body is conceived of as a whole, and the different substances of which, to a superficial observer, it appears to be composed — the blood, flesh, sinews — like the elements out of which they are formed, are supposed to pass into one another in regular order, while the infinite complexity of the human frame remains unobserved. And diseases arise from the opposite process — when the natural proportions of the four elements are disturbed, and the secondary substances which are formed out of them, namely, blood, flesh, sinews, are generated in an inverse order.

Plato found heat and air within the human frame, and the blood circulating in every part. He assumes in language almost unintelligible to us that a network of fire and air envelopes the greater part of the body. This outer net contains two lesser nets, one corresponding to the stomach, the other to the lungs; and the entrance to the latter is forked or divided into two passages which lead to the nostrils and to the mouth. In the process of respiration the external net is said to find a way in and out of the pores of the skin: while the interior of it and the lesser nets move alternately into each other. The whole description is figurative, as Plato himself implies when he speaks of a 'fountain of fire which we compare to the network of a creel.' He really means by this what we should describe as a state of heat or temperature in the interior of the body. The 'fountain of fire' or heat is also in a figure the circulation of the blood. The passage is partly imagination, partly fact.

He has a singular theory of respiration for which he accounts solely by the movement of the air in and out of the body; he does not attribute any part of the process to the action of the body itself. The air has a double ingress and a double exit, through the mouth or nostrils, and through the skin. When exhaled through the mouth or nostrils, it leaves a vacuum which is filled up by other air finding a way in through the pores, this air being thrust out of its place by the exhalation from the mouth and nostrils. There is also a corresponding process of inhalation through the mouth or nostrils, and of exhalation through the pores. The inhalation through the pores appears to take place nearly at the same time as the exhalation through the mouth; and conversely. The internal fire is in either case the propelling cause outwards — the inhaled air, when heated by it, having a natural tendency to move out of the body to the place of fire; while the impossibility of a vacuum is the propelling cause inwards.

Thus we see that this singular theory is dependent on two principles largely employed by Plato in explaining the operations of nature, the impossibility of a vacuum and the attraction of like to like. To these there has to be added a third principle, which is the condition of the action of the other two — the interpenetration of particles in proportion to their density or rarity. It is this which enables fire and air to permeate the flesh.

Plato's account of digestion and the circulation of the blood is closely connected with his theory of respiration. Digestion is supposed to be effected by the action of the internal fire, which in the process of respiration moves into the stomach and minces the food. As the fire returns to its place, it takes with it the minced food or blood; and in this way the veins are replenished. Plato does not enquire how the blood is separated from the faeces.

Of the anatomy and functions of the body he knew very little — e.g. of the uses of the nerves in conveying motion and sensation, which he supposed to be communicated by the bones and veins; he was also ignorant of the distinction between veins and arteries; — the latter term he applies to the vessels which conduct air from the mouth to the lungs; — he supposes the lung to be hollow and bloodless; the spinal marrow he conceives to be the seed of generation; he confuses the parts of the body with the states of the body — the network of fire and air is spoken of as a bodily organ; he has absolutely no idea of the phenomena of respiration, which he attributes to a law of equalization in nature, the air which is breathed out displacing other air which finds a way in; he is wholly unacquainted with the process of digestion. Except the general divisions into the spleen, the liver, the belly, and the lungs, and the obvious distinctions of flesh, bones, and the limbs of the body, we find nothing that reminds us of anatomical facts. But we find much which is derived from his theory of the universe, and transferred to man, as there is much also in his theory of the universe which is suggested by man. The microcosm of the human body is the lesser image of the macrocosm. The courses of the same and the other affect both; they are made of the same elements and therefore in the same proportions. Both are intelligent natures endued with the power of self-motion, and the same equipoise is maintained in both. The animal is a sort of 'world' to the particles of the blood which circulate in it. All the four elements entered into the original composition of the human frame; the bone was formed out of smooth earth; liquids of various kinds pass to and fro; the network of fire and air irrigates the veins. Infancy and childhood is the chaos or first turbid flux of sense prior to the establishment of order; the intervals of time which may be observed in some intermittent fevers correspond to the density of the elements. The spinal marrow, including the brain, is formed out of the finest sorts of triangles, and is the connecting link between body and mind. Health is only to be preserved by imitating the motions of the world in space, which is the mother and nurse of generation. The work of digestion is carried on by the superior sharpness of the triangles forming the substances of the human body to those which are introduced into it in the shape of food. The freshest and acutest forms of triangles are those that are found in children, but they become more obtuse with advancing years; and when they finally wear out and fall to pieces, old age and death supervene.

As in the Republic, Plato is still the enemy of the purgative treatment of physicians, which, except in extreme cases, no man of sense will ever adopt. For, as he adds, with an insight into the truth, 'every disease is akin to the nature of the living being and is only irritated by stimulants.' He is of opinion that nature should be left to herself, and is inclined to think that physicians are in vain (Laws — where he says that warm baths would be more beneficial to the limbs of the aged rustic than the prescriptions of a not over-wise doctor). If he seems to be extreme in his condemnation of medicine and to rely too much on diet and exercise, he might appeal to nearly all the best physicians of our own age in support of his opinions, who often speak to their patients of the worthlessness of drugs. For we ourselves are sceptical about medicine, and very unwilling to submit to the purgative treatment of physicians. May we not claim for Plato an anticipation of modern ideas as about some questions of astronomy and physics, so also about medicine? As in the Charmides he tells us that the body cannot be cured without the soul, so in the Timaeus he strongly asserts the sympathy of soul and body; any defect of either is the occasion of the greatest discord and disproportion in the other. Here too may be a presentiment that in the medicine of the future the interdependence of mind and body will be more fully recognized, and that the influence of the one over the other may be exerted in a manner which is not now thought possible.

Section 7.

In Plato's explanation of sensation we are struck by the fact that he has not the same distinct conception of organs of sense which is familiar to ourselves. The senses are not instruments, but rather passages, through which external objects strike upon the mind. The eye is the aperture through which the stream of vision passes, the ear is the aperture through which the vibrations of sound pass. But that the complex structure of the eye or the ear is in any sense the cause of sight and hearing he seems hardly to be aware.

The process of sight is the most complicated (Rep.), and consists of three elements — the light which is supposed to reside within the eye, the light of the sun, and the light emitted from external objects. When the light of the eye meets the light of the sun, and both together meet the light issuing from an external object, this is the simple act of sight. When the particles of light which proceed from the object are exactly equal to the particles of the visual ray which meet them from within, then the body is transparent. If they are larger and contract the visual ray, a black colour is produced; if they are smaller and dilate it, a white. Other phenomena are produced by the variety and motion of light. A sudden flash of fire at once elicits light and moisture from the eye, and causes a bright colour. A more subdued light, on mingling with the moisture of the eye, produces a red colour. Out of these elements all other colours are derived. All of them are combinations of bright and red with white and black. Plato himself tells us that he does not know in what proportions they combine, and he is of opinion that such knowledge is granted to the gods only. To have seen the affinity of them to each other and their connection with light, is not a bad basis for a theory of colours. We must remember that they were not distinctly defined to his, as they are to our eyes; he saw them, not as they are divided in the prism, or artificially manufactured for the painter's use, but as they exist in nature, blended and confused with one another.

We can hardly agree with him when he tells us that smells do not admit of kinds. He seems to think that no definite qualities can attach to bodies which are in a state of transition or evaporation; he also makes the subtle observation that smells must be denser than air, though thinner than water, because when there is an obstruction to the breathing, air can penetrate, but not smell.

The affections peculiar to the tongue are of various kinds, and, like many other affections, are caused by contraction and dilation. Some of them are produced by rough, others by abstergent, others by inflammatory substances — these act upon the testing instruments of the tongue, and produce a more or less disagreeable sensation, while other particles congenial to the tongue soften and harmonize them. The instruments of taste reach from the tongue to the heart. Plato has a lively sense of the manner in which sensation and motion are communicated from one part of the body to the other, though he confuses the affections with the organs. Hearing is a blow which passes through the ear and ends in the region of the liver, being transmitted by means of the air, the brain, and the blood to the soul. The swifter sound is acute, the sound which moves slowly is grave. A great body of sound is loud, the opposite is low. Discord is produced by the swifter and slower motions of two sounds, and is converted into harmony when the swifter motions begin to pause and are overtaken by the slower.

The general phenomena of sensation are partly internal, but the more violent are caused by conflict with external objects. Proceeding by a method of superficial observation, Plato remarks that the more sensitive parts of the human frame are those which are least covered by flesh, as is the case with the head and the elbows. Man, if his head had been covered with a thicker pulp of flesh, might have been a longer-lived animal than he is, but could not have had as quick perceptions. On the other hand, the tongue is one of the most sensitive of organs; but then this is made, not to be a covering to the bones which contain the marrow or source of life, but with an express purpose, and in a separate mass.

Section 8.

We have now to consider how far in any of these speculations Plato approximated to the discoveries of modern science. The modern physical philosopher is apt to dwell exclusively on the absurdities of ancient ideas about science, on the haphazard fancies and a priori assumptions of ancient teachers, on their confusion of facts and ideas, on their inconsistency and blindness to the most obvious phenomena. He measures them not by what preceded them, but by what has followed them. He does not consider that ancient physical philosophy was not a free enquiry, but a growth, in which the mind was passive rather than active, and was incapable of resisting the impressions which flowed in upon it. He hardly allows to the notions of the ancients the merit of being the stepping-stones by which he has himself risen to a higher knowledge. He never reflects, how great a thing it was to have formed a conception, however imperfect, either of the human frame as a whole, or of the world as a whole. According to the view taken in these volumes the errors of ancient physicists were not separable from the intellectual conditions under which they lived. Their genius was their own; and they were not the rash and hasty generalizers which, since the days of Bacon, we have been apt to suppose them. The thoughts of men widened to receive experience; at first they seemed to know all things as in a dream: after a while they look at them closely and hold them in their hands. They begin to arrange them in classes and to connect causes with effects. General notions are necessary to the apprehension of particular facts, the metaphysical to the physical. Before men can observe the world, they must be able to conceive it.

To do justice to the subject, we should consider the physical philosophy of the ancients as a whole; we should remember, (1) that the nebular theory was the received belief of several of the early physicists; (2) that the development of animals out of fishes who came to land, and of man out of the animals, was held by Anaximander in the sixth century before Christ (Plut. Symp. Quaest; Plac. Phil.); (3) that even by Philolaus and the early Pythagoreans, the earth was held to be a body like the other stars revolving in space around the sun or a central fire; (4) that the beginnings of chemistry are discernible in the 'similar particles' of Anaxagoras. Also they knew or thought (5) that there was a sex in plants as well as in animals; (6) they were aware that musical notes depended on the relative length or tension of the strings from which they were emitted, and were measured by ratios of number; (7) that mathematical laws pervaded the world; and even qualitative differences were supposed to have their origin in number and figure; (8) the annihilation of matter was denied by several of them, and the seeming disappearance of it held to be a transformation only. For, although one of these discoveries might have been supposed to be a happy guess, taken together they seem to imply a great advance and almost maturity of natural knowledge.

We should also remember, when we attribute to the ancients hasty generalizations and delusions of language, that physical philosophy and metaphysical too have been guilty of similar fallacies in quite recent times. We by no means distinguish clearly between mind and body, between ideas and facts. Have not many discussions arisen about the Atomic theory in which a point has been confused with a material atom? Have not the natures of things been explained by imaginary entities, such as life or phlogiston, which exist in the mind only? Has not disease been regarded, like sin, sometimes as a negative and necessary, sometimes as a positive or malignant principle? The 'idols' of Bacon are nearly as common now as ever; they are inherent in the human mind, and when they have the most complete dominion over us, we are least able to perceive them. We recognize them in the ancients, but we fail to see them in ourselves.

Such reflections, although this is not the place in which to dwell upon them at length, lead us to take a favourable view of the speculations of the Timaeus. We should consider not how much Plato actually knew, but how far he has contributed to the general ideas of physics, or supplied the notions which, whether true or false, have stimulated the minds of later generations in the path of discovery. Some of them may seem old-fashioned, but may nevertheless have had a great influence in promoting system and assisting enquiry, while in others we hear the latest word of physical or metaphysical philosophy. There is also an intermediate class, in which Plato falls short of the truths of modern science, though he is not wholly unacquainted with them. (1) To the first class belongs the teleological theory of creation. Whether all things in the world can be explained as the result of natural laws, or whether we must not admit of tendencies and marks of design also, has been a question much disputed of late years. Even if all phenomena are the result of natural forces, we must admit that there are many things in heaven and earth which are as well expressed under the image of mind or design as under any other. At any rate, the language of Plato has been the language of natural theology down to our own time, nor can any description of the world wholly dispense with it. The notion of first and second or co-operative causes, which originally appears in the Timaeus, has likewise survived to our own day, and has been a great peace- maker between theology and science. Plato also approaches very near to our doctrine of the primary and secondary qualities of matter. (2) Another popular notion which is found in the Timaeus, is the feebleness of the human intellect —'God knows the original qualities of things; man can only hope to attain to probability.' We speak in almost the same words of human intelligence, but not in the same manner of the uncertainty of our knowledge of nature. The reason is that the latter is assured to us by experiment, and is not contrasted with the certainty of ideal or mathematical knowledge. But the ancient philosopher never experimented: in the Timaeus Plato seems to have thought that there would be impiety in making the attempt; he, for example, who tried experiments in colours would 'forget the difference of the human and divine natures.' Their indefiniteness is probably the reason why he singles them out, as especially incapable of being tested by experiment. (Compare the saying of Anaxagoras — Sext. Pyrrh. — that since snow is made of water and water is black, snow ought to be black.)

The greatest 'divination' of the ancients was the supremacy which they assigned to mathematics in all the realms of nature; for in all of them there is a foundation of mechanics. Even physiology partakes of figure and number; and Plato is not wrong in attributing them to the human frame, but in the omission to observe how little could be explained by them. Thus we may remark in passing that the most fanciful of ancient philosophies is also the most nearly verified in fact. The fortunate guess that the world is a sum of numbers and figures has been the most fruitful of anticipations. The 'diatonic' scale of the Pythagoreans and Plato suggested to Kepler that the secret of the distances of the planets from one another was to be found in mathematical proportions. The doctrine that the heavenly bodies all move in a circle is known by us to be erroneous; but without such an error how could the human mind have comprehended the heavens? Astronomy, even in modern times, has made far greater progress by the high a priori road than could have been attained by any other. Yet, strictly speaking — and the remark applies to ancient physics generally — this high a priori road was based upon a posteriori grounds. For there were no facts of which the ancients were so well assured by experience as facts of number. Having observed that they held good in a few instances, they applied them everywhere; and in the complexity, of which they were capable, found the explanation of the equally complex phenomena of the universe. They seemed to see them in the least things as well as in the greatest; in atoms, as well as in suns and stars; in the human body as well as in external nature. And now a favourite speculation of modern chemistry is the explanation of qualitative difference by quantitative, which is at present verified to a certain extent and may hereafter be of far more universal application. What is this but the atoms of Democritus and the triangles of Plato? The ancients should not be wholly deprived of the credit of their guesses because they were unable to prove them. May they not have had, like the animals, an instinct of something more than they knew?

Besides general notions we seem to find in the Timaeus some more precise approximations to the discoveries of modern physical science. First, the doctrine of equipoise. Plato affirms, almost in so many words, that nature abhors a vacuum. Whenever a particle is displaced, the rest push and thrust one another until equality is restored. We must remember that these ideas were not derived from any definite experiment, but were the original reflections of man, fresh from the first observation of nature. The latest word of modern philosophy is continuity and development, but to Plato this is the beginning and foundation of science; there is nothing that he is so strongly persuaded of as that the world is one, and that all the various existences which are contained in it are only the transformations of the same soul of the world acting on the same matter. He would have readily admitted that out of the protoplasm all things were formed by the gradual process of creation; but he would have insisted that mind and intelligence — not meaning by this, however, a conscious mind or person — were prior to them, and could alone have created them. Into the workings of this eternal mind or intelligence he does not enter further; nor would there have been any use in attempting to investigate the things which no eye has seen nor any human language can express.

Lastly, there remain two points in which he seems to touch great discoveries of modern times — the law of gravitation, and the circulation of the blood.

(1) The law of gravitation, according to Plato, is a law, not only of the attraction of lesser bodies to larger ones, but of similar bodies to similar, having a magnetic power as well as a principle of gravitation. He observed that earth, water, and air had settled down to their places, and he imagined fire or the exterior aether to have a place beyond air. When air seemed to go upwards and fire to pierce through air — when water and earth fell downward, they were seeking their native elements. He did not remark that his own explanation did not suit all phenomena; and the simpler explanation, which assigns to bodies degrees of heaviness and lightness proportioned to the mass and distance of the bodies which attract them, never occurred to him. Yet the affinities of similar substances have some effect upon the composition of the world, and of this Plato may be thought to have had an anticipation. He may be described as confusing the attraction of gravitation with the attraction of cohesion. The influence of such affinities and the chemical action of one body upon another in long periods of time have become a recognized principle of geology.

(2) Plato is perfectly aware — and he could hardly be ignorant — that blood is a fluid in constant motion. He also knew that blood is partly a solid substance consisting of several elements, which, as he might have observed in the use of 'cupping-glasses', decompose and die, when no longer in motion. But the specific discovery that the blood flows out on one side of the heart through the arteries and returns through the veins on the other, which is commonly called the circulation of the blood, was absolutely unknown to him.

A further study of the Timaeus suggests some after-thoughts which may be conveniently brought together in this place. The topics which I propose briefly to reconsider are (a) the relation of the Timaeus to the other dialogues of Plato and to the previous philosophy; (b) the nature of God and of creation (c) the morality of the Timaeus:—

(a) The Timaeus is more imaginative and less scientific than any other of the Platonic dialogues. It is conjectural astronomy, conjectural natural philosophy, conjectural medicine. The writer himself is constantly repeating that he is speaking what is probable only. The dialogue is put into the mouth of Timaeus, a Pythagorean philosopher, and therefore here, as in the Parmenides, we are in doubt how far Plato is expressing his own sentiments. Hence the connexion with the other dialogues is comparatively slight. We may fill up the lacunae of the Timaeus by the help of the Republic or Phaedrus: we may identify the same and other with the (Greek) of the Philebus. We may find in the Laws or in the Statesman parallels with the account of creation and of the first origin of man. It would be possible to frame a scheme in which all these various elements might have a place. But such a mode of proceeding would be unsatisfactory, because we have no reason to suppose that Plato intended his scattered thoughts to be collected in a system. There is a common spirit in his writings, and there are certain general principles, such as the opposition of the sensible and intellectual, and the priority of mind, which run through all of them; but he has no definite forms of words in which he consistently expresses himself. While the determinations of human thought are in process of creation he is necessarily tentative and uncertain. And there is least of definiteness, whenever either in describing the beginning or the end of the world, he has recourse to myths. These are not the fixed modes in which spiritual truths are revealed to him, but the efforts of imagination, by which at different times and in various manners he seeks to embody his conceptions. The clouds of mythology are still resting upon him, and he has not yet pierced 'to the heaven of the fixed stars' which is beyond them. It is safer then to admit the inconsistencies of the Timaeus, or to endeavour to fill up what is wanting from our own imagination, inspired by a study of the dialogue, than to refer to other Platonic writings — and still less should we refer to the successors of Plato — for the elucidation of it.

More light is thrown upon the Timaeus by a comparison of the previous philosophies. For the physical science of the ancients was traditional, descending through many generations of Ionian and Pythagorean philosophers. Plato does not look out upon the heavens and describe what he sees in them, but he builds upon the foundations of others, adding something out of the 'depths of his own self-consciousness.' Socrates had already spoken of God the creator, who made all things for the best. While he ridiculed the superficial explanations of phenomena which were current in his age, he recognised the marks both of benevolence and of design in the frame of man and in the world. The apparatus of winds and waters is contemptuously rejected by him in the Phaedo, but he thinks that there is a power greater than that of any Atlas in the 'Best' (Phaedo; Arist. Met.). Plato, following his master, affirms this principle of the best, but he acknowledges that the best is limited by the conditions of matter. In the generation before Socrates, Anaxagoras had brought together 'Chaos' and 'Mind'; and these are connected by Plato in the Timaeus, but in accordance with his own mode of thinking he has interposed between them the idea or pattern according to which mind worked. The circular impulse (Greek) of the one philosopher answers to the circular movement (Greek) of the other. But unlike Anaxagoras, Plato made the sun and stars living beings and not masses of earth or metal. The Pythagoreans again had framed a world out of numbers, which they constructed into figures. Plato adopted their speculations and improved upon them by a more exact knowledge of geometry. The Atomists too made the world, if not out of geometrical figures, at least out of different forms of atoms, and these atoms resembled the triangles of Plato in being too small to be visible. But though the physiology of the Timaeus is partly borrowed from them, they are either ignored by Plato or referred to with a secret contempt and dislike. He looks with more favour on the Pythagoreans, whose intervals of number applied to the distances of the planets reappear in the Timaeus. It is probable that among the Pythagoreans living in the fourth century B.C., there were already some who, like Plato, made the earth their centre. Whether he obtained his circles of the Same and Other from any previous thinker is uncertain. The four elements are taken from Empedocles; the interstices of the Timaeus may also be compared with his (Greek). The passage of one element into another is common to Heracleitus and several of the Ionian philosophers. So much of a syncretist is Plato, though not after the manner of the Neoplatonists. For the elements which he borrows from others are fused and transformed by his own genius. On the other hand we find fewer traces in Plato of early Ionic or Eleatic speculation.

He does not imagine the world of sense to be made up of opposites or to be in a perpetual flux, but to vary within certain limits which are controlled by what he calls the principle of the same. Unlike the Eleatics, who relegated the world to the sphere of not-being, he admits creation to have an existence which is real and even eternal, although dependent on the will of the creator. Instead of maintaining the doctrine that the void has a necessary place in the existence of the world, he rather affirms the modern thesis that nature abhors a vacuum, as in the Sophist he also denies the reality of not-being (Aristot. Metaph.). But though in these respects he differs from them, he is deeply penetrated by the spirit of their philosophy; he differs from them with reluctance, and gladly recognizes the 'generous depth' of Parmenides (Theaet.).

There is a similarity between the Timaeus and the fragments of Philolaus, which by some has been thought to be so great as to create a suspicion that they are derived from it. Philolaus is known to us from the Phaedo of Plato as a Pythagorean philosopher residing at Thebes in the latter half of the fifth century B.C., after the dispersion of the original Pythagorean society. He was the teacher of Simmias and Cebes, who became disciples of Socrates. We have hardly any other information about him. The story that Plato had purchased three books of his writings from a relation is not worth repeating; it is only a fanciful way in which an ancient biographer dresses up the fact that there was supposed to be a resemblance between the two writers. Similar gossiping stories are told about the sources of the Republic and the Phaedo. That there really existed in antiquity a work passing under the name of Philolaus there can be no doubt. Fragments of this work are preserved to us, chiefly in Stobaeus, a few in Boethius and other writers. They remind us of the Timaeus, as well as of the Phaedrus and Philebus. When the writer says (Stob. Eclog.) that all things are either finite (definite) or infinite (indefinite), or a union of the two, and that this antithesis and synthesis pervades all art and nature, we are reminded of the Philebus. When he calls the centre of the world (Greek), we have a parallel to the Phaedrus. His distinction between the world of order, to which the sun and moon and the stars belong, and the world of disorder, which lies in the region between the moon and the earth, approximates to Plato's sphere of the Same and of the Other. Like Plato (Tim.), he denied the above and below in space, and said that all things were the same in relation to a centre. He speaks also of the world as one and indestructible: 'for neither from within nor from without does it admit of destruction' (Tim). He mentions ten heavenly bodies, including the sun and moon, the earth and the counter-earth (Greek), and in the midst of them all he places the central fire, around which they are moving — this is hidden from the earth by the counter-earth. Of neither is there any trace in Plato, who makes the earth the centre of his system. Philolaus magnifies the virtues of particular numbers, especially of the number 10 (Stob. Eclog.), and descants upon odd and even numbers, after the manner of the later Pythagoreans. It is worthy of remark that these mystical fancies are nowhere to be found in the writings of Plato, although the importance of number as a form and also an instrument of thought is ever present to his mind. Both Philolaus and Plato agree in making the world move in certain numerical ratios according to a musical scale: though Bockh is of opinion that the two scales, of Philolaus and of the Timaeus, do not correspond . . . We appear not to be sufficiently acquainted with the early Pythagoreans to know how far the statements contained in these fragments corresponded with their doctrines; and we therefore cannot pronounce, either in favour of the genuineness of the fragments, with Bockh and Zeller, or, with Valentine Rose and Schaarschmidt, against them. But it is clear that they throw but little light upon the Timaeus, and that their resemblance to it has been exaggerated.

That there is a degree of confusion and indistinctness in Plato's account both of man and of the universe has been already acknowledged. We cannot tell (nor could Plato himself have told) where the figure or myth ends and the philosophical truth begins; we cannot explain (nor could Plato himself have explained to us) the relation of the ideas to appearance, of which one is the copy of the other, and yet of all things in the world they are the most opposed and unlike. This opposition is presented to us in many forms, as the antithesis of the one and many, of the finite and infinite, of the intelligible and sensible, of the unchangeable and the changing, of the indivisible and the divisible, of the fixed stars and the planets, of the creative mind and the primeval chaos. These pairs of opposites are so many aspects of the great opposition between ideas and phenomena — they easily pass into one another; and sometimes the two members of the relation differ in kind, sometimes only in degree. As in Aristotle's matter and form the connexion between them is really inseparable; for if we attempt to separate them they become devoid of content and therefore indistinguishable; there is no difference between the idea of which nothing can be predicated, and the chaos or matter which has no perceptible qualities — between Being in the abstract and Nothing. Yet we are frequently told that the one class of them is the reality and the other appearance; and one is often spoken of as the double or reflection of the other. For Plato never clearly saw that both elements had an equal place in mind and in nature; and hence, especially when we argue from isolated passages in his writings, or attempt to draw what appear to us to be the natural inferences from them, we are full of perplexity. There is a similar confusion about necessity and free- will, and about the state of the soul after death. Also he sometimes supposes that God is immanent in the world, sometimes that he is transcendent. And having no distinction of objective and subjective, he passes imperceptibly from one to the other; from intelligence to soul, from eternity to time. These contradictions may be softened or concealed by a judicious use of language, but they cannot be wholly got rid of. That an age of intellectual transition must also be one of inconsistency; that the creative is opposed to the critical or defining habit of mind or time, has been often repeated by us. But, as Plato would say, 'there is no harm in repeating twice or thrice' (Laws) what is important for the understanding of a great author.

It has not, however, been observed, that the confusion partly arises out of the elements of opposing philosophies which are preserved in him. He holds these in solution, he brings them into relation with one another, but he does not perfectly harmonize them. They are part of his own mind, and he is incapable of placing himself outside of them and criticizing them. They grow as he grows; they are a kind of composition with which his own philosophy is overlaid. In early life he fancies that he has mastered them: but he is also mastered by them; and in language (Sophist) which may be compared with the hesitating tone of the Timaeus, he confesses in his later years that they are full of obscurity to him. He attributes new meanings to the words of Parmenides and Heracleitus; but at times the old Eleatic philosophy appears to go beyond him; then the world of phenomena disappears, but the doctrine of ideas is also reduced to nothingness. All of them are nearer to one another than they themselves supposed, and nearer to him than he supposed. All of them are antagonistic to sense and have an affinity to number and measure and a presentiment of ideas. Even in Plato they still retain their contentious or controversial character, which was developed by the growth of dialectic. He is never able to reconcile the first causes of the pre-Socratic philosophers with the final causes of Socrates himself. There is no intelligible account of the relation of numbers to the universal ideas, or of universals to the idea of good. He found them all three, in the Pythagorean philosophy and in the teaching of Socrates and of the Megarians respectively; and, because they all furnished modes of explaining and arranging phenomena, he is unwilling to give up any of them, though he is unable to unite them in a consistent whole.

Lastly, Plato, though an idealist philosopher, is Greek and not Oriental in spirit and feeling. He is no mystic or ascetic; he is not seeking in vain to get rid of matter or to find absorption in the divine nature, or in the Soul of the universe. And therefore we are not surprised to find that his philosophy in the Timaeus returns at last to a worship of the heavens, and that to him, as to other Greeks, nature, though containing a remnant of evil, is still glorious and divine. He takes away or drops the veil of mythology, and presents her to us in what appears to him to be the form- fairer and truer far — of mathematical figures. It is this element in the Timaeus, no less than its affinity to certain Pythagorean speculations, which gives it a character not wholly in accordance with the other dialogues of Plato.

(b) The Timaeus contains an assertion perhaps more distinct than is found in any of the other dialogues (Rep.; Laws) of the goodness of God. 'He was good himself, and he fashioned the good everywhere.' He was not 'a jealous God,' and therefore he desired that all other things should be equally good. He is the IDEA of good who has now become a person, and speaks and is spoken of as God. Yet his personality seems to appear only in the act of creation. In so far as he works with his eye fixed upon an eternal pattern he is like the human artificer in the Republic. Here the theory of Platonic ideas intrudes upon us. God, like man, is supposed to have an ideal of which Plato is unable to tell us the origin. He may be said, in the language of modern philosophy, to resolve the divine mind into subject and object.

The first work of creation is perfected, the second begins under the direction of inferior ministers. The supreme God is withdrawn from the world and returns to his own accustomed nature (Tim.). As in the Statesman, he retires to his place of view. So early did the Epicurean doctrine take possession of the Greek mind, and so natural is it to the heart of man, when he has once passed out of the stage of mythology into that of rational religion. For he sees the marks of design in the world; but he no longer sees or fancies that he sees God walking in the garden or haunting stream or mountain. He feels also that he must put God as far as possible out of the way of evil, and therefore he banishes him from an evil world. Plato is sensible of the difficulty; and he often shows that he is desirous of justifying the ways of God to man. Yet on the other hand, in the Tenth Book of the Laws he passes a censure on those who say that the Gods have no care of human things.

The creation of the world is the impression of order on a previously existing chaos. The formula of Anaxagoras — 'all things were in chaos or confusion, and then mind came and disposed them' — is a summary of the first part of the Timaeus. It is true that of a chaos without differences no idea could be formed. All was not mixed but one; and therefore it was not difficult for the later Platonists to draw inferences by which they were enabled to reconcile the narrative of the Timaeus with the Mosaic account of the creation. Neither when we speak of mind or intelligence, do we seem to get much further in our conception than circular motion, which was deemed to be the most perfect. Plato, like Anaxagoras, while commencing his theory of the universe with ideas of mind and of the best, is compelled in the execution of his design to condescend to the crudest physics.

(c) The morality of the Timaeus is singular, and it is difficult to adjust the balance between the two elements of it. The difficulty which Plato feels, is that which all of us feel, and which is increased in our own day by the progress of physical science, how the responsibility of man is to be reconciled with his dependence on natural causes. And sometimes, like other men, he is more impressed by one aspect of human life, sometimes by the other. In the Republic he represents man as freely choosing his own lot in a state prior to birth — a conception which, if taken literally, would still leave him subject to the dominion of necessity in his after life; in the Statesman he supposes the human race to be preserved in the world only by a divine interposition; while in the Timaeus the supreme God commissions the inferior deities to avert from him all but self-inflicted evils — words which imply that all the evils of men are really self-inflicted. And here, like Plato (the insertion of a note in the text of an ancient writer is a literary curiosity worthy of remark), we may take occasion to correct an error. For we too hastily said that Plato in the Timaeus regarded all 'vices and crimes as involuntary.' But the fact is that he is inconsistent with himself; in one and the same passage vice is attributed to the relaxation of the bodily frame, and yet we are exhorted to avoid it and pursue virtue. It is also admitted that good and evil conduct are to be attributed respectively to good and evil laws and institutions. These cannot be given by individuals to themselves; and therefore human actions, in so far as they are dependent upon them, are regarded by Plato as involuntary rather than voluntary. Like other writers on this subject, he is unable to escape from some degree of self-contradiction. He had learned from Socrates that vice is ignorance, and suddenly the doctrine seems to him to be confirmed by observing how much of the good and bad in human character depends on the bodily constitution. So in modern times the speculative doctrine of necessity has often been supported by physical facts.

The Timaeus also contains an anticipation of the stoical life according to nature. Man contemplating the heavens is to regulate his erring life according to them. He is to partake of the repose of nature and of the order of nature, to bring the variable principle in himself into harmony with the principle of the same. The ethics of the Timaeus may be summed up in the single idea of 'law.' To feel habitually that he is part of the order of the universe, is one of the highest ethical motives of which man is capable. Something like this is what Plato means when he speaks of the soul 'moving about the same in unchanging thought of the same.' He does not explain how man is acted upon by the lesser influences of custom or of opinion; or how the commands of the soul watching in the citadel are conveyed to the bodily organs. But this perhaps, to use once more expressions of his own, 'is part of another subject' or 'may be more suitably discussed on some other occasion.'

There is no difficulty, by the help of Aristotle and later writers, in criticizing the Timaeus of Plato, in pointing out the inconsistencies of the work, in dwelling on the ignorance of anatomy displayed by the author, in showing the fancifulness or unmeaningness of some of his reasons. But the Timaeus still remains the greatest effort of the human mind to conceive the world as a whole which the genius of antiquity has bequeathed to us.

…

One more aspect of the Timaeus remains to be considered — the mythological or geographical. Is it not a wonderful thing that a few pages of one of Plato's dialogues have grown into a great legend, not confined to Greece only, but spreading far and wide over the nations of Europe and reaching even to Egypt and Asia? Like the tale of Troy, or the legend of the Ten Tribes (Ewald, Hist. of Isr.), which perhaps originated in a few verses of II Esdras, it has become famous, because it has coincided with a great historical fact. Like the romance of King Arthur, which has had so great a charm, it has found a way over the seas from one country and language to another. It inspired the navigators of the fifteenth and sixteenth centuries; it foreshadowed the discovery of America. It realized the fiction so natural to the human mind, because it answered the enquiry about the origin of the arts, that there had somewhere existed an ancient primitive civilization. It might find a place wherever men chose to look for it; in North, South, East, or West; in the Islands of the Blest; before the entrance of the Straits of Gibraltar, in Sweden or in Palestine. It mattered little whether the description in Plato agreed with the locality assigned to it or not. It was a legend so adapted to the human mind that it made a habitation for itself in any country. It was an island in the clouds, which might be seen anywhere by the eye of faith. It was a subject especially congenial to the ponderous industry of certain French and Swedish writers, who delighted in heaping up learning of all sorts but were incapable of using it.

M. Martin has written a valuable dissertation on the opinions entertained respecting the Island of Atlantis in ancient and modern times. It is a curious chapter in the history of the human mind. The tale of Atlantis is the fabric of a vision, but it has never ceased to interest mankind. It was variously regarded by the ancients themselves. The stronger heads among them, like Strabo and Longinus, were as little disposed to believe in the truth of it as the modern reader in Gulliver or Robinson Crusoe. On the other hand there is no kind or degree of absurdity or fancy in which the more foolish writers, both of antiquity and of modern times, have not indulged respecting it. The Neo-Platonists, loyal to their master, like some commentators on the Christian Scriptures, sought to give an allegorical meaning to what they also believed to be an historical fact. It was as if some one in our own day were to convert the poems of Homer into an allegory of the Christian religion, at the same time maintaining them to be an exact and veritable history. In the Middle Ages the legend seems to have been half-forgotten until revived by the discovery of America. It helped to form the Utopia of Sir Thomas More and the New Atlantis of Bacon, although probably neither of those great men were at all imposed upon by the fiction. It was most prolific in the seventeenth or in the early part of the eighteenth century, when the human mind, seeking for Utopias or inventing them, was glad to escape out of the dulness of the present into the romance of the past or some ideal of the future. The later forms of such narratives contained features taken from the Edda, as well as from the Old and New Testament; also from the tales of missionaries and the experiences of travellers and of colonists.

The various opinions respecting the Island of Atlantis have no interest for us except in so far as they illustrate the extravagances of which men are capable. But this is a real interest and a serious lesson, if we remember that now as formerly the human mind is liable to be imposed upon by the illusions of the past, which are ever assuming some new form.

When we have shaken off the rubbish of ages, there remain one or two questions of which the investigation has a permanent value:—

1. Did Plato derive the legend of Atlantis from an Egyptian source? It may be replied that there is no such legend in any writer previous to Plato; neither in Homer, nor in Pindar, nor in Herodotus is there any mention of an Island of Atlantis, nor any reference to it in Aristotle, nor any citation of an earlier writer by a later one in which it is to be found. Nor have any traces been discovered hitherto in Egyptian monuments of a connexion between Greece and Egypt older than the eighth or ninth century B.C. It is true that Proclus, writing in the fifth century after Christ, tells us of stones and columns in Egypt on which the history of the Island of Atlantis was engraved. The statement may be false — there are similar tales about columns set up 'by the Canaanites whom Joshua drove out' (Procop.); but even if true, it would only show that the legend, 800 years after the time of Plato, had been transferred to Egypt, and inscribed, not, like other forgeries, in books, but on stone. Probably in the Alexandrian age, when Egypt had ceased to have a history and began to appropriate the legends of other nations, many such monuments were to be found of events which had become famous in that or other countries. The oldest witness to the story is said to be Crantor, a Stoic philosopher who lived a generation later than Plato, and therefore may have borrowed it from him. The statement is found in Proclus; but we require better assurance than Proclus can give us before we accept this or any other statement which he makes.

Secondly, passing from the external to the internal evidence, we may remark that the story is far more likely to have been invented by Plato than to have been brought by Solon from Egypt. That is another part of his legend which Plato also seeks to impose upon us. The verisimilitude which he has given to the tale is a further reason for suspecting it; for he could easily 'invent Egyptian or any other tales' (Phaedrus). Are not the words, 'The truth of the story is a great advantage,' if we read between the lines, an indication of the fiction? It is only a legend that Solon went to Egypt, and if he did he could not have conversed with Egyptian priests or have read records in their temples. The truth is that the introduction is a mosaic work of small touches which, partly by their minuteness, and also by their seeming probability, win the confidence of the reader. Who would desire better evidence than that of Critias, who had heard the narrative in youth when the memory is strongest at the age of ten from his grandfather Critias, an old man of ninety, who in turn had heard it from Solon himself? Is not the famous expression —'You Hellenes are ever children and there is no knowledge among you hoary with age,' really a compliment to the Athenians who are described in these words as 'ever young'? And is the thought expressed in them to be attributed to the learning of the Egyptian priest, and not rather to the genius of Plato? Or when the Egyptian says — 'Hereafter at our leisure we will take up the written documents and examine in detail the exact truth about these things'— what is this but a literary trick by which Plato sets off his narrative? Could any war between Athens and the Island of Atlantis have really coincided with the struggle between the Greeks and Persians, as is sufficiently hinted though not expressly stated in the narrative of Plato? And whence came the tradition to Egypt? or in what does the story consist except in the war between the two rival powers and the submersion of both of them? And how was the tale transferred to the poem of Solon? 'It is not improbable,' says Mr. Grote, 'that Solon did leave an unfinished Egyptian poem' (Plato). But are probabilities for which there is not a tittle of evidence, and which are without any parallel, to be deemed worthy of attention by the critic? How came the poem of Solon to disappear in antiquity? or why did Plato, if the whole narrative was known to him, break off almost at the beginning of it?

While therefore admiring the diligence and erudition of M. Martin, we cannot for a moment suppose that the tale was told to Solon by an Egyptian priest, nor can we believe that Solon wrote a poem upon the theme which was thus suggested to him — a poem which disappeared in antiquity; or that the Island of Atlantis or the antediluvian Athens ever had any existence except in the imagination of Plato. Martin is of opinion that Plato would have been terrified if he could have foreseen the endless fancies to which his Island of Atlantis has given occasion. Rather he would have been infinitely amused if he could have known that his gift of invention would have deceived M. Martin himself into the belief that the tradition was brought from Egypt by Solon and made the subject of a poem by him. M. Martin may also be gently censured for citing without sufficient discrimination ancient authors having very different degrees of authority and value.

2. It is an interesting and not unimportant question which is touched upon by Martin, whether the Atlantis of Plato in any degree held out a guiding light to the early navigators. He is inclined to think that there is no real connexion between them. But surely the discovery of the New World was preceded by a prophetic anticipation of it, which, like the hope of a Messiah, was entering into the hearts of men? And this hope was nursed by ancient tradition, which had found expression from time to time in the celebrated lines of Seneca and in many other places. This tradition was sustained by the great authority of Plato, and therefore the legend of the Island of Atlantis, though not closely connected with the voyages of the early navigators, may be truly said to have contributed indirectly to the great discovery.

The Timaeus of Plato, like the Protagoras and several portions of the Phaedrus and Republic, was translated by Cicero into Latin. About a fourth, comprehending with lacunae the first portion of the dialogue, is preserved in several MSS. These generally agree, and therefore may be supposed to be derived from a single original. The version is very faithful, and is a remarkable monument of Cicero's skill in managing the difficult and intractable Greek. In his treatise De Natura Deorum, he also refers to the Timaeus, which, speaking in the person of Velleius the Epicurean, he severely criticises.

The commentary of Proclus on the Timaeus is a wonderful monument of the silliness and prolixity of the Alexandrian Age. It extends to about thirty pages of the book, and is thirty times the length of the original. It is surprising that this voluminous work should have found a translator (Thomas Taylor, a kindred spirit, who was himself a Neo-Platonist, after the fashion, not of the fifth or sixteenth, but of the nineteenth century A.D.). The commentary is of little or no value, either in a philosophical or philological point of view. The writer is unable to explain particular passages in any precise manner, and he is equally incapable of grasping the whole. He does not take words in their simple meaning or sentences in their natural connexion. He is thinking, not of the context in Plato, but of the contemporary Pythagorean philosophers and their wordy strife. He finds nothing in the text which he does not bring to it. He is full of Porphyry, Iamblichus and Plotinus, of misapplied logic, of misunderstood grammar, and of the Orphic theology.

Although such a work can contribute little or nothing to the understanding of Plato, it throws an interesting light on the Alexandrian times; it realizes how a philosophy made up of words only may create a deep and widespread enthusiasm, how the forms of logic and rhetoric may usurp the place of reason and truth, how all philosophies grow faded and discoloured, and are patched and made up again like worn-out garments, and retain only a second-hand existence. He who would study this degeneracy of philosophy and of the Greek mind in the original cannot do better than devote a few of his days and nights to the commentary of Proclus on the Timaeus.

A very different account must be given of the short work entitled 'Timaeus Locrus,' which is a brief but clear analysis of the Timaeus of Plato, omitting the introduction or dialogue and making a few small additions. It does not allude to the original from which it is taken; it is quite free from mysticism and Neo-

Platonism. In length it does not exceed a fifth part of the Timaeus. It is written in the Doric dialect, and contains several words which do not occur in classical Greek. No other indication of its date, except this uncertain one of language, appears in it. In several places the writer has simplified the language of Plato, in a few others he has embellished and exaggerated it. He generally preserves the thought of the original, but does not copy the words. On the whole this little tract faithfully reflects the meaning and spirit of the Timaeus.

>From the garden of the Timaeus, as from the other dialogues of Plato, we may still gather a few flowers and present them at parting to the reader. There is nothing in Plato grander and simpler than the conversation between Solon and the Egyptian priest, in which the youthfulness of Hellas is contrasted with the antiquity of Egypt. Here are to be found the famous words, 'O Solon, Solon, you Hellenes are ever young, and there is not an old man among you'— which may be compared to the lively saying of Hegel, that 'Greek history began with the youth Achilles and left off with the youth Alexander.' The numerous arts of verisimilitude by which Plato insinuates into the mind of the reader the truth of his narrative have been already referred to. Here occur a sentence or two not wanting in Platonic irony (Greek — a word to the wise). 'To know or tell the origin of the other divinities is beyond us, and we must accept the traditions of the men of old time who affirm themselves to be the offspring of the Gods — that is what they say — and they must surely have known their own ancestors. How can we doubt the word of the children of the Gods? Although they give no probable or certain proofs, still, as they declare that they are speaking of what took place in their own family, we must conform to custom and believe them.' 'Our creators well knew that women and other animals would some day be framed out of men, and they further knew that many animals would require the use of nails for many purposes; wherefore they fashioned in men at their first creation the rudiments of nails.' Or once more, let us reflect on two serious passages in which the order of the world is supposed to find a place in the human soul and to infuse harmony into it. 'The soul, when touching anything that has essence, whether dispersed in parts or undivided, is stirred through all her powers to declare the sameness or difference of that thing and some other; and to what individuals are related, and by what affected, and in what way and how and when, both in the world of generation and in the world of immutable being. And when reason, which works with equal truth, whether she be in the circle of the diverse or of the same — in voiceless silence holding her onward course in the sphere of the self-moved — when reason, I say, is hovering around the sensible world, and when the circle of the diverse also moving truly imparts the intimations of sense to the whole soul, then arise opinions and beliefs sure and certain. But when reason is concerned with the rational, and the circle of the same moving smoothly declares it, then intelligence and knowledge are necessarily perfected;' where, proceeding in a similar path of contemplation, he supposes the inward and the outer world mutually to imply each other. 'God invented and gave us sight to the end that we might behold the courses of intelligence in the heaven, and apply them to the courses of our own intelligence which are akin to them, the unperturbed to the perturbed; and that we, learning them and partaking of the natural truth of reason, might imitate the absolutely unerring courses of God and regulate our own vagaries.' Or let us weigh carefully some other profound thoughts, such as the following. 'He who neglects education walks lame to the end of his life, and returns imperfect and good for nothing to the world below.' 'The father and maker of all this universe is past finding out; and even if we found him, to tell of him to all men would be impossible.' 'Let me tell you then why the Creator made this world of generation. He was good, and the good can never have jealousy of anything. And being free from jealousy, he desired that all things should be as like himself as they could be. This is in the truest sense the origin of creation and of the world, as we shall do well in believing on the testimony of wise men: God desired that all things should be good and nothing bad, so far as this was attainable.' This is the leading thought in the Timaeus, just as the IDEA of Good is the leading thought of the Republic, the one expression describing the personal, the other the impersonal Good or God, differing in form rather than in substance, and both equally implying to the mind of Plato a divine reality. The slight touch, perhaps ironical, contained in the words, 'as we shall do well in believing on the testimony of wise men,' is very characteristic of Plato.

Timaeus

PERSONS OF THE DIALOGUE: Socrates, Critias, Timaeus, Hermocrates.

SOCRATES: One, two, three; but where, my dear Timaeus, is the fourth of those who were yesterday my guests and are to be my entertainers to-day?

TIMAEUS: He has been taken ill, Socrates; for he would not willingly have been absent from this gathering.

SOCRATES: Then, if he is not coming, you and the two others must supply his place.

TIMAEUS: Certainly, and we will do all that we can; having been handsomely entertained by you yesterday, those of us who remain should be only too glad to return your hospitality.

SOCRATES: Do you remember what were the points of which I required you to speak?

TIMAEUS: We remember some of them, and you will be here to remind us of anything which we have forgotten: or rather, if we are not troubling you, will you briefly recapitulate the whole, and then the particulars will be more firmly fixed in our memories?

SOCRATES: To be sure I will: the chief theme of my yesterday's discourse was the State — how constituted and of what citizens composed it would seem likely to be most perfect.

TIMAEUS: Yes, Socrates; and what you said of it was very much to our mind.

SOCRATES: Did we not begin by separating the husbandmen and the artisans from the class of defenders of the State?

TIMAEUS: Yes.

SOCRATES: And when we had given to each one that single employment and particular art which was suited to his nature, we spoke of those who were intended to be our warriors, and said that they were to be guardians of the city against attacks from within as well as from without, and to have no other employment; they were to be merciful in judging their subjects, of whom they were by nature friends, but fierce to their enemies, when they came across them in battle.

TIMAEUS: Exactly.

SOCRATES: We said, if I am not mistaken, that the guardians should be gifted with a temperament in a high degree both passionate and philosophical; and that then they would be as they ought to be, gentle to their friends and fierce with their enemies.

TIMAEUS: Certainly.

SOCRATES: And what did we say of their education? Were they not to be trained in gymnastic, and music, and all other sorts of knowledge which were proper for them?

TIMAEUS: Very true.

SOCRATES: And being thus trained they were not to consider gold or silver or anything else to be their own private property; they were to be like hired troops, receiving pay for keeping guard from those who were protected by them — the pay was to be no more than would suffice for men of simple life; and they were to spend in common, and to live together in the continual practice of virtue, which was to be their sole pursuit.

TIMAEUS: That was also said.

SOCRATES: Neither did we forget the women; of whom we declared, that their natures should be assimilated and brought into harmony with those of the men, and that common pursuits should be assigned to them both in time of war and in their ordinary life.

TIMAEUS: That, again, was as you say.

SOCRATES: And what about the procreation of children? Or rather was not the proposal too singular to be forgotten? for all wives and children were to be in common, to the intent that no one should ever know his own child, but they were to imagine that they were all one family; those who were within a suitable limit of age were to be brothers and sisters, those who were of an elder generation parents and grandparents, and those of a younger, children and grandchildren.

TIMAEUS: Yes, and the proposal is easy to remember, as you say.

SOCRATES: And do you also remember how, with a view of securing as far as we could the best breed, we said that the chief magistrates, male and female, should contrive secretly, by the use of certain lots, so to arrange the nuptial meeting, that the bad of either sex and the good of either sex might pair with their like; and there was to be no quarrelling on this account, for they would imagine that the union was a mere accident, and was to be attributed to the lot?

TIMAEUS: I remember.

SOCRATES: And you remember how we said that the children of the good parents were to be educated, and the children of the bad secretly dispersed among the inferior citizens; and while they were all growing up the rulers were to be on the look-out, and to bring up from below in their turn those who were worthy, and those among themselves who were unworthy were to take the places of those who came up?

TIMAEUS: True.

SOCRATES: Then have I now given you all the heads of our yesterday's discussion? Or is there anything more, my dear Timaeus, which has been omitted?

TIMAEUS: Nothing, Socrates; it was just as you have said.

SOCRATES: I should like, before proceeding further, to tell you how I feel about the State which we have described. I might compare myself to a person who, on beholding beautiful animals either created by the painter's art, or, better still, alive but at rest, is seized with a desire of seeing them in motion or engaged in some struggle or conflict to which their forms appear suited; this is my feeling about the State which we have been describing. There are conflicts which all cities undergo, and I should like to hear some one tell of our own city carrying on a struggle against her neighbours, and how she went out to war in a becoming manner, and when at war showed by the greatness of her actions and the magnanimity of her words in dealing with other cities a result worthy of her training and education. Now I, Critias and Hermocrates, am conscious that I myself should never be able to celebrate the city and her citizens in a befitting manner, and I am not surprised at my own incapacity; to me the wonder is rather that the poets present as well as past are no better — not that I mean to depreciate them; but every one can see that they are a tribe of imitators, and will imitate best and most easily the life in which they have been brought up; while that which is beyond the range of a man's education he finds hard to carry out in action, and still harder adequately to represent in language. I am aware that the Sophists have plenty of brave words and fair conceits, but I am afraid that being only wanderers from one city to another, and having never had habitations of their own, they may fail in their conception of philosophers and statesmen, and may not know what they do and say in time of war, when they are fighting or holding parley with their enemies. And thus people of your class are the only ones remaining who are fitted by nature and education to take part at once both in politics and philosophy. Here is Timaeus, of Locris in Italy, a city which has admirable laws, and who is himself in wealth and rank the equal of any of his fellow-citizens; he has held the most important and honourable offices in his own state, and, as I believe, has scaled the heights of all philosophy; and here is Critias, whom every Athenian knows to be no novice in the matters of which we are speaking; and as to Hermocrates, I am assured by many witnesses that his genius and education qualify him to take part in any speculation of the kind. And therefore yesterday when I saw that you wanted me to describe the formation of the State, I readily assented, being very well aware, that, if you only would, none were better qualified to carry the discussion further, and that when you had engaged our city in a suitable war, you of all men living could best exhibit her playing a fitting part. When I had completed my task, I in return imposed this other task upon you. You conferred together and agreed to entertain me to-day, as I had entertained you, with a feast of discourse. Here am I in festive array, and no man can be more ready for the promised banquet.

HERMOCRATES: And we too, Socrates, as Timaeus says, will not be wanting in enthusiasm; and there is no excuse for not complying with your request. As soon as we arrived yesterday at the guest-chamber of Critias, with whom we are staying, or rather on our way thither, we talked the matter over, and he told us an ancient tradition, which I wish, Critias, that you would repeat to Socrates, so that he may help us to judge whether it will satisfy his requirements or not.

CRITIAS: I will, if Timaeus, who is our other partner, approves.

TIMAEUS: I quite approve.

CRITIAS: Then listen, Socrates, to a tale which, though strange, is certainly true, having been attested by Solon, who was the wisest of the seven sages. He was a relative and a dear friend of my great-grandfather, Dropides, as he himself says in many passages of his poems; and he told the story to Critias, my grandfather, who remembered and repeated it to us. There were of old, he said, great and marvellous actions of the Athenian city, which have passed into oblivion through lapse of time and the destruction of mankind, and one in particular, greater than all the rest. This we will now rehearse. It will be a fitting monument of our gratitude to you, and a hymn of praise true and worthy of the goddess, on this her day of festival.

SOCRATES: Very good. And what is this ancient famous action of the Athenians, which Critias declared, on the authority of Solon, to be not a mere legend, but an actual fact?

CRITIAS: I will tell an old-world story which I heard from an aged man; for Critias, at the time of telling it, was, as he said, nearly ninety years of age, and I was about ten. Now the day was that day of the Apaturia which is called the Registration of Youth, at which, according to custom, our parents gave prizes for recitations, and the poems of several poets were recited by us boys, and many of us sang the poems of

Solon, which at that time had not gone out of fashion. One of our tribe, either because he thought so or to please Critias, said that in his judgment Solon was not only the wisest of men, but also the noblest of poets. The old man, as I very well remember, brightened up at hearing this and said, smiling: Yes, Amynander, if Solon had only, like other poets, made poetry the business of his life, and had completed the tale which he brought with him from Egypt, and had not been compelled, by reason of the factions and troubles which he found stirring in his own country when he came home, to attend to other matters, in my opinion he would have been as famous as Homer or Hesiod, or any poet.

And what was the tale about, Critias? said Amynander.

About the greatest action which the Athenians ever did, and which ought to have been the most famous, but, through the lapse of time and the destruction of the actors, it has not come down to us.

Tell us, said the other, the whole story, and how and from whom Solon heard this veritable tradition.

He replied:— In the Egyptian Delta, at the head of which the river Nile divides, there is a certain district which is called the district of Sais, and the great city of the district is also called Sais, and is the city from which King Amasis came. The citizens have a deity for their foundress; she is called in the Egyptian tongue Neith, and is asserted by them to be the same whom the Hellenes call Athene; they are great lovers of the Athenians, and say that they are in some way related to them. To this city came Solon, and was received there with great honour; he asked the priests who were most skilful in such matters, about antiquity, and made the discovery that neither he nor any other Hellene knew anything worth mentioning about the times of old. On one occasion, wishing to draw them on to speak of antiquity, he began to tell about the most ancient things in our part of the world — about Phoroneus, who is called 'the first man,' and about Niobe; and after the Deluge, of the survival of Deucalion and Pyrrha; and he traced the genealogy of their descendants, and reckoning up the dates, tried to compute how many years ago the events of which he was speaking happened. Thereupon one of the priests, who was of a very great age, said: O Solon, Solon, you Hellenes are never anything but children, and there is not an old man among you. Solon in return asked him what he meant. I mean to say, he replied, that in mind you are all young; there is no old opinion handed down among you by ancient tradition, nor any science which is hoary with age. And I will tell you why. There have been, and will be again, many destructions of mankind arising out of many causes; the greatest have been brought about by the agencies of fire and water, and other lesser ones by innumerable other causes. There is a story, which even you have preserved, that once upon a time Paethon, the son of Helios, having yoked the steeds in his father's chariot, because he was not able to drive them in the path of his father, burnt up all that was upon the earth, and was himself destroyed by a thunderbolt. Now this has the form of a myth, but really signifies a declination of the bodies moving in the heavens around the earth, and a great conflagration of things upon the earth, which recurs after long intervals; at such times those who live upon the mountains and in dry and lofty places are more liable to destruction than those who dwell by rivers or on the seashore. And from this calamity the Nile, who is our never-failing saviour, delivers and preserves us. When, on the other hand, the gods purge the earth with a deluge of water, the survivors in your country are herdsmen and shepherds who dwell on the mountains, but those who, like you, live in cities are carried by the rivers into the sea. Whereas in this land, neither then nor at any other time, does the water come down from above on the fields, having always a tendency to come up from below; for which reason the traditions preserved here are the most ancient. The fact is, that wherever the extremity of winter frost or of summer sun does not prevent, mankind exist, sometimes in greater, sometimes in lesser numbers. And whatever happened either in your country or in ours, or in any other region of which we are informed — if there were any actions noble or great or in any other way remarkable, they have all been written down by us of old, and are preserved in our temples. Whereas just when you and other nations are beginning to be provided with letters and the other requisites of civilized life, after the usual interval, the stream from heaven, like a pestilence, comes pouring down, and leaves only those of you who are destitute of letters and education; and so you have to begin all over again like children, and know nothing of what happened in ancient times, either among us or among yourselves. As for those genealogies of yours which you just now recounted to us, Solon, they are no better than the tales of children. In the first place you remember a single deluge only, but there were many previous ones; in the next place, you do not know that there formerly dwelt in your land the fairest and noblest race of men which ever lived, and that you and your whole city are descended from a small seed or remnant of them which survived. And this was unknown to you, because, for many generations, the survivors of that destruction died, leaving no written word. For there was a time, Solon, before the great deluge of all, when the city which now is Athens was first in war and in every way the best governed of all cities, is said to have performed the noblest deeds and to have had the fairest constitution of any of which tradition tells, under the face of heaven. Solon marvelled at his words, and earnestly requested the priests to inform him exactly and in order about these former citizens. You are welcome to hear about them, Solon, said the priest, both for your own sake and for that of your city, and above all, for the sake of the goddess who is the common patron and parent and educator of both our cities. She founded your city a thousand years before ours (Observe that Plato gives the same date (9000 years ago) for the foundation of Athens and for the repulse of the invasion from Atlantis (Crit.).), receiving from the Earth and Hephaestus the seed of your race, and afterwards she founded ours, of which the constitution is recorded in our sacred registers to be 8000 years old. As touching your citizens of 9000 years ago, I will briefly inform you of their laws and of their most famous action; the exact particulars of the whole we will hereafter go through at our leisure in the sacred registers themselves. If you compare these very laws with ours you will find that many of ours are the counterpart of yours as they were in the olden time. In the first place, there is the caste of priests, which is separated from all the others; next, there are the artificers, who ply their several crafts by themselves and do not intermix; and also there is the class of shepherds and of hunters, as well as that of husbandmen; and you will observe, too, that the warriors in Egypt are distinct from all the other classes, and are commanded by the law to devote themselves solely to military pursuits; moreover, the weapons which they carry are shields and spears, a style of equipment which the goddess taught of Asiatics first to us, as in your part of the world first to you. Then as to wisdom, do you observe how our law from the very first made a study of the whole order of things, extending even to prophecy and medicine which gives health, out of these divine elements deriving what was needful for human life, and adding every sort of knowledge which was akin to them. All this order and arrangement the goddess first imparted to you when establishing your city; and she chose the spot of earth in which you were born, because she saw that the happy temperament of the seasons in that land would produce the wisest of men. Wherefore the goddess, who was a lover both of war and of wisdom, selected and first of all settled that spot which was the most likely to produce men likest herself. And there you dwelt, having such laws as these and still better ones, and excelled all mankind in all virtue, as became the children and disciples of the gods.

Many great and wonderful deeds are recorded of your state in our histories. But one of them exceeds all the rest in greatness and valour. For these histories tell of a mighty power which unprovoked made an expedition against the whole of Europe and Asia, and to which your city put an end. This power came forth out of the Atlantic Ocean, for in those days the Atlantic was navigable; and there was an island situated in front of the straits which are by you called the Pillars of Heracles; the island was larger than Libya and Asia put together, and was the way to other islands, and from these you might pass to the whole of the opposite continent which surrounded the true ocean; for this sea which is within the Straits of Heracles is only a harbour, having a narrow entrance, but that other is a real sea, and the surrounding land may be most truly called a boundless continent. Now in this island of Atlantis there was a great and wonderful empire which had rule over the whole island and several others, and over parts of the continent, and, furthermore, the men of Atlantis had subjected the parts of Libya within the columns of Heracles as far as Egypt, and of Europe as far as Tyrrhenia. This vast power, gathered into one, endeavoured to subdue at a blow our country and yours and the whole of the region within the straits; and then, Solon, your country shone forth, in the excellence of her virtue and strength, among all mankind. She was pre-eminent in courage and military skill, and was the leader of the Hellenes. And when the rest fell off from her, being compelled to stand alone, after having undergone the very extremity of danger, she defeated and triumphed over the invaders, and preserved from slavery those who were not yet subjugated, and generously liberated all the rest of us who dwell within the pillars. But afterwards there occurred violent earthquakes and floods; and in a single day and night of misfortune all your warlike men in a body sank into the earth, and the island of Atlantis in like manner disappeared in the depths of the sea. For which reason the sea in those parts is impassable and impenetrable, because there is a shoal of mud in the way; and this was caused by the subsidence of the island.

I have told you briefly, Socrates, what the aged Critias heard from Solon and related to us. And when you were speaking yesterday about your city and citizens, the tale which I have just been repeating to you came into my mind, and I remarked with astonishment how, by some mysterious coincidence, you agreed in almost every particular with the narrative of Solon; but I did not like to speak at the moment. For a long time had elapsed, and I had forgotten too much; I thought that I must first of all run over the narrative in my own mind, and then I would speak. And so I readily assented to your request yesterday, considering that in all such cases the chief difficulty is to find a tale suitable to our purpose, and that with such a tale we should be fairly well provided.

And therefore, as Hermocrates has told you, on my way home yesterday I at once communicated the tale to my companions as I remembered it; and after I left them, during the night by thinking I recovered nearly the whole of it. Truly, as is often said, the lessons of our childhood make a wonderful impression on our memories; for I am not sure that I could remember all the discourse of yesterday, but I should be much surprised if I forgot any of these things which I have heard very long ago. I listened at the time with childlike interest to the old man's narrative; he was very ready to teach me, and I asked him again and again to repeat his words, so that like an indelible picture they were branded into my mind. As soon as the day broke, I rehearsed them as he spoke them to my companions, that they, as well as myself, might have something to say. And now, Socrates, to make an end of my preface, I am ready to tell you the whole tale. I will give you not only the general heads, but the particulars, as they were told to me. The city and citizens, which you yesterday described to us in fiction, we will now transfer to the world of reality. It shall be the ancient city of Athens, and we will suppose that the citizens whom you imagined, were our veritable ancestors, of whom the priest spoke; they will perfectly harmonize, and there will be no inconsistency in saying that the citizens of your republic are these ancient Athenians. Let us divide the subject among us, and all endeavour according to our ability gracefully to execute the task which you have imposed upon us. Consider then, Socrates, if this narrative is suited to the purpose, or whether we should seek for some other instead.

SOCRATES: And what other, Critias, can we find that will be better than this, which is natural and suitable to the festival of the goddess, and has the very great advantage of being a fact and not a fiction? How or where shall we find another if we abandon this? We cannot, and therefore you must tell the tale, and good luck to you; and I in return for my yesterday's discourse will now rest and be a listener.

CRITIAS: Let me proceed to explain to you, Socrates, the order in which we have arranged our entertainment. Our intention is, that Timaeus, who is the most of an astronomer amongst us, and has made the nature of the universe his special study, should speak first, beginning with the generation of the world and going down to the creation of man; next, I am to receive the men whom he has created, and of whom some will have profited by the excellent education which you have given them; and then, in accordance with the tale of Solon, and equally with his law, we will bring them into court and make them citizens, as if they were those very Athenians whom the sacred Egyptian record has recovered from oblivion, and thenceforward we will speak of them as Athenians and fellow-citizens.

SOCRATES: I see that I shall receive in my turn a perfect and splendid feast of reason. And now, Timaeus, you, I suppose, should speak next, after duly calling upon the Gods.

TIMAEUS: All men, Socrates, who have any degree of right feeling, at the beginning of every enterprise, whether small or great, always call upon God. And we, too, who are going to discourse of the nature of the universe, how created or how existing without creation, if we be not altogether out of our wits, must invoke the aid of Gods and Goddesses and pray that our words may be acceptable to them and consistent with themselves. Let this, then, be our invocation of the Gods, to which I add an exhortation of myself to speak in such manner as will be most intelligible to you, and will most accord with my own intent.

First then, in my judgment, we must make a distinction and ask, What is that which always is and has no becoming; and what is that which is always becoming and never is? That which is apprehended by intelligence and reason is always in the same state; but that which is conceived by opinion with the help of sensation and without reason, is always in a process of becoming and perishing and never really is. Now everything that becomes or is created must of necessity be created by some cause, for without a cause nothing can be created. The work of the creator, whenever he looks to the unchangeable and fashions the form and nature of his work after an unchangeable pattern, must necessarily be made fair and perfect; but when he looks to the created only, and uses a created pattern, it is not fair or perfect. Was the heaven then or the world, whether called by this or by any other more appropriate name — assuming the name, I am asking a question which has to be asked at the beginning of an enquiry about anything — was the world, I say, always in existence and without beginning? or created, and had it a beginning? Created, I reply, being visible and tangible and having a body, and therefore sensible; and all sensible things are apprehended by opinion and sense and are in a process of creation and created. Now that which is created must, as we affirm, of necessity be created by a cause. But the father and maker of all this universe is past finding out; and even if we found him, to tell of him to all men would be impossible. And there is still a question to be asked about him: Which of the patterns had the artificer in view when he made the world — the pattern of the unchangeable, or of that which is created? If the world be indeed fair and the artificer good, it is manifest that he must have looked to that which is eternal; but if what cannot be said without blasphemy is true, then to the created pattern. Every one will see that he must have looked to the eternal; for the world is the fairest of creations and he is the best of causes. And having been created in this way, the world has been framed in the likeness of that which is apprehended by reason and mind and is unchangeable, and must therefore of necessity, if this is admitted, be a copy of something. Now it is all-important that the beginning of everything should be according to nature. And in speaking of the copy and the original we may assume that words are akin to the matter which they describe; when they relate to the lasting and permanent and intelligible, they ought to be lasting and unalterable, and, as far as their nature allows, irrefutable and immovable — nothing less. But when they express only the copy or likeness and not the eternal things themselves, they need only be likely and analogous to the real words. As being is to becoming, so is truth to belief. If then, Socrates, amid the many opinions about the gods and the generation of the universe, we are not able to give notions which are altogether and in every respect exact and consistent with one another, do not be surprised. Enough, if we adduce probabilities as likely as any others; for we must remember that I who am the speaker, and you who are the judges, are only mortal men, and we ought to accept the tale which is probable and enquire no further.

SOCRATES: Excellent, Timaeus; and we will do precisely as you bid us. The prelude is charming, and is already accepted by us — may we beg of you to proceed to the strain?

TIMAEUS: Let me tell you then why the creator made this world of generation. He was good, and the good can never have any jealousy of anything. And being free from jealousy, he desired that all things should be as like himself as they could be. This is in the truest sense the origin of creation and of the world, as we shall do well in believing on the testimony of wise men: God desired that all things should be good and nothing bad, so far as this was attainable. Wherefore also finding the whole visible sphere not at rest, but moving in an irregular and disorderly fashion, out of disorder he brought order, considering that this was in every way better than the other. Now the deeds of the best could never be or have been other than the fairest; and the creator, reflecting on the things which are by nature visible, found that no unintelligent creature taken as a whole was fairer than the intelligent taken as a whole; and that intelligence could not be present in anything which was devoid of soul. For which reason, when he was framing the universe, he put intelligence in soul, and soul in body, that he might be the creator of a work which was by nature fairest and best. Wherefore, using the language of probability, we may say that the world became a living creature truly endowed with soul and intelligence by the providence of God.

This being supposed, let us proceed to the next stage: In the likeness of what animal did the Creator make the world? It would be an unworthy thing to liken it to any nature which exists as a part only; for nothing can be beautiful which is like any imperfect thing; but let us suppose the world to be the very image of that whole of which all other animals both individually and in their tribes are portions. For the original of the universe contains in itself all intelligible beings, just as this world comprehends us and all other visible creatures. For the Deity, intending to make this world like the fairest and most perfect of intelligible beings, framed one visible animal comprehending within itself all other animals of a kindred nature. Are we right in saying that there is one world, or that they are many and infinite? There must be one only, if the created copy is to accord with the original. For that which includes all other intelligible creatures cannot have a second or companion; in that case there would be need of another living being which would include both, and of which they would be parts, and the likeness would be more truly said to resemble not them, but that other which included them. In order then that the world might be solitary, like the perfect animal, the creator made not two worlds or an infinite number of them; but there is and ever will be one only-begotten and created heaven.

Now that which is created is of necessity corporeal, and also visible and tangible. And nothing is visible where there is no fire, or tangible which has no solidity, and nothing is solid without earth. Wherefore also God in the beginning of creation made the body of the universe to consist of fire and earth. But two things cannot be rightly put together without a third; there must be some bond of union between them. And the fairest bond is that which makes the most complete fusion of itself and the things which it combines; and proportion is best adapted to effect such a union. For whenever in any three numbers, whether cube or square, there is a mean, which is to the last term what the first term is to it; and again, when the mean is to the first term as the last term is to the mean — then the mean becoming first and last, and the first and last both becoming means, they will all of them of necessity come to be the same, and having become the same with one another will be all one. If the universal frame had been created a surface only and having no depth, a single mean would have sufficed to bind together itself and the other terms; but now, as the world must be solid, and solid bodies are always compacted not by one mean but by two, God placed water and air in the mean between fire and earth, and made them to have the same proportion so far as was possible (as fire is to air so is air to water, and as air is to water so is water to earth); and thus he bound and put together a visible and tangible heaven. And for these reasons, and out of such elements which are in number four, the body of the world was created, and it was harmonized by proportion, and therefore has the spirit of friendship; and having been reconciled to itself, it was indissoluble by the hand of any other than the framer.

Now the creation took up the whole of each of the four elements; for the Creator compounded the world out of all the fire and all the water and all the air and all the earth, leaving no part of any of them nor any power of them outside. His intention was, in the first place, that the animal should be as far as possible a perfect whole and of perfect parts: secondly, that it should be one, leaving no remnants out of which another such world might be created: and also that it should be free from old age and unaffected by disease. Considering that if heat and cold and other powerful forces which unite bodies surround and attack them from without when they are unprepared, they decompose them, and by bringing diseases and old age upon them, make them waste away — for this cause and on these grounds he made the world one whole, having every part entire, and being therefore perfect and not liable to old age and disease. And he gave to the world the figure which was suitable and also natural. Now to the animal which was to comprehend all animals, that figure was suitable which comprehends within itself all other figures. Wherefore he made the world in the form of a globe, round as from a lathe, having its extremes in every direction equidistant from the centre, the most perfect and the most like itself of all figures; for he considered that the like is infinitely fairer than the unlike. This he finished off, making the surface smooth all round for many reasons; in the first place, because the living being had no need of eyes when there was nothing remaining outside him to be seen; nor of ears when there was nothing to be heard; and there was no surrounding atmosphere to be breathed; nor would there have been any use of organs by the help of which he might receive his food or get rid of what he had already digested, since there was nothing which went from him or came into him: for there was nothing beside him. Of design he was created thus, his own waste providing his own food, and all that he did or suffered taking place in and by himself. For the Creator conceived that a being which was self-sufficient would be far more excellent than one which lacked anything; and, as he had no need to take anything or defend himself against any one, the Creator did not think it necessary to bestow upon him hands: nor had he any need of feet, nor of the whole apparatus of walking; but the movement suited to his spherical form was assigned to him, being of all the seven that which is most appropriate to mind and intelligence; and he was made to move in the same manner and on the same spot, within his own limits revolving in a circle. All the other six motions were taken away from him, and he was made not to partake of their deviations. And as this circular movement required no feet, the universe was created without legs and without feet.

Such was the whole plan of the eternal God about the god that was to be, to whom for this reason he gave a body, smooth and even, having a surface in every direction equidistant from the centre, a body entire and perfect, and formed out of perfect bodies. And in the centre he put the soul, which he diffused throughout the body, making it also to be the exterior environment of it; and he made the universe a circle moving in a circle, one and solitary, yet by reason of its excellence able to converse with itself, and needing no other friendship or acquaintance. Having these purposes in view he created the world a blessed god.

Now God did not make the soul after the body, although we are speaking of them in this order; for having brought them together he would never have allowed that the elder should be ruled by the younger; but this is a random manner of speaking which we have, because somehow we ourselves too are very much under the dominion of chance. Whereas he made the soul in origin and excellence prior to and older than the body, to be the ruler and mistress, of whom the body was to be the subject. And he made her out of the following elements and on this wise: Out of the indivisible and unchangeable, and also out of that which is divisible and has to do with material bodies, he compounded a third and intermediate kind of essence, partaking of the nature of the same and of the other, and this compound he placed accordingly in a mean between the indivisible, and the divisible and material. He took the three elements of the same, the other, and the essence, and mingled them into one form, compressing by force the reluctant and unsociable nature of the other into the same. When he had mingled them with the essence and out of three made one, he again divided this whole into as many portions as was fitting, each portion being a compound of the same, the other, and the essence. And he proceeded to divide after this manner:— First of all, he took away one part of the whole (1), and then he separated a second part which was double the first (2), and then he took away a third part which was half as much again as the second and three times as much as the first (3), and then he took a fourth part which was twice as much as the second (4), and a fifth part which was three times the third (9), and a sixth part which was eight times the first (8), and a seventh part which was twenty-seven times the first (27). After this he filled up the double intervals (i.e. between 1, 2, 4, 8) and the triple (i.e. between 1, 3, 9, 27) cutting off yet other portions from the mixture and placing them in the intervals, so that in each interval there were two kinds of means, the one exceeding and exceeded by equal parts of its extremes (as for example 1, 4/3, 2, in which the mean 4/3 is one-third of 1 more than 1, and one-third of 2 less than 2), the other being that kind of mean which exceeds and is exceeded by an equal number (e.g.

— over 1, 4/3, 3/2, — over 2, 8/3, 3, — over 4, 16/3, 6, — over 8: and — over 1, 3/2, 2, — over 3, 9/2, 6, — over 9, 27/2, 18, — over 27.).

Where there were intervals of 3/2 and of 4/3 and of 9/8, made by the connecting terms in the former intervals, he filled up all the intervals of 4/3 with the interval of 9/8, leaving a fraction over; and the interval which this fraction expressed was in the ratio of 256 to 243 (e.g.

243:256::81/64:4/3::243/128:2::81/32:8/3::243/64:4::81/16:16/3::242/32:8.).

And thus the whole mixture out of which he cut these portions was all exhausted by him. This entire compound he divided lengthways into two parts, which he joined to one another at the centre like the letter X, and bent them into a circular form, connecting them with themselves and each other at the point opposite to their original meeting-point; and, comprehending them in a uniform revolution upon the same axis, he made the one the outer and the other the inner circle. Now the motion of the outer circle he called the motion of the same, and the motion of the inner circle the motion of the other or diverse. The motion of the same he carried round by the side (i.e. of the rectangular figure supposed to be inscribed in the circle of the Same) to the right, and the motion of the diverse diagonally (i.e. across the rectangular figure from corner to corner) to the left. And he gave dominion to the motion of the same and like, for that he left single and undivided; but the inner motion he divided in six places and made seven unequal circles having their intervals in ratios of two and three, three of each, and bade the orbits proceed in a direction opposite to one another; and three (Sun, Mercury, Venus) he made to move with equal swiftness, and the remaining four (Moon, Saturn, Mars, Jupiter) to move with unequal swiftness to the three and to one another, but in due proportion.

Now when the Creator had framed the soul according to his will, he formed within her the corporeal universe, and brought the two together, and united them centre to centre. The soul, interfused everywhere from the centre to the circumference of heaven, of which also she is the external envelopment, herself turning in herself, began a divine beginning of never-ceasing and rational life enduring throughout all time. The body of heaven is visible, but the soul is invisible, and partakes of reason and harmony, and being made by the best of intellectual and everlasting natures, is the best of things created. And because she is composed of the same and of the other and of the essence, these three, and is divided and united in due proportion, and in her revolutions returns upon herself, the soul, when touching anything which has essence, whether dispersed in parts or undivided, is stirred through all her powers, to declare the sameness or difference of that thing and some other; and to what individuals are related, and by what affected, and in what way and how and when, both in the world of generation and in the world of immutable being. And when reason, which works with equal truth, whether she be in the circle of the diverse or of the same — in voiceless silence holding her onward course in the sphere of the self-moved — when reason, I say, is hovering around the sensible world and when the circle of the diverse also moving truly imparts the intimations of sense to the whole soul, then arise opinions and beliefs sure and certain. But when reason is concerned with the rational, and the circle of the same moving smoothly declares it, then intelligence and knowledge are necessarily perfected. And if any one affirms that in which these two are found to be other than the soul, he will say the very opposite of the truth.

When the father and creator saw the creature which he had made moving and living, the created image of the eternal gods, he rejoiced, and in his joy determined to make the copy still more like the original; and as this was eternal, he sought to make the universe eternal, so far as might be. Now the nature of the ideal being was everlasting, but to bestow this attribute in its fulness upon a creature was impossible. Wherefore he resolved to have a moving image of eternity, and when he set in order the heaven, he made this image eternal but moving according to number, while eternity itself rests in unity; and this image we call time. For there were no days and nights and months and years before the heaven was created, but when he constructed the heaven he created them also. They are all parts of time, and the past and future are created species of time, which we unconsciously but wrongly transfer to the eternal essence; for we say that he 'was,' he 'is,' he 'will be,' but the truth is that 'is' alone is properly attributed to him, and that 'was' and 'will be' are only to be spoken of becoming in time, for they are motions, but that which is immovably the same cannot become older or younger by time, nor ever did or has become, or hereafter will be, older or younger, nor is subject at all to any of those states which affect moving and sensible things and of which generation is the cause. These are the forms of time, which imitates eternity and revolves according to a law of number. Moreover, when we say that what has become IS become and what becomes IS becoming, and that what will become IS about to become and that the non-existent IS non-existent — all these are inaccurate modes of expression (compare Parmen.). But perhaps this whole subject will be more suitably discussed on some other occasion.

Time, then, and the heaven came into being at the same instant in order that, having been created together, if ever there was to be a dissolution of them, they might be dissolved together. It was framed after the pattern of the eternal nature, that it might resemble this as far as was possible; for the pattern exists from eternity, and the created heaven has been, and is, and will be, in all time. Such was the mind and thought of God in the creation of time. The sun and moon and five other stars, which are called the planets, were created by him in order to distinguish and preserve the numbers of time; and when he had made their several bodies, he placed them in the orbits in which the circle of the other was revolving — in seven orbits seven stars. First, there was the moon in the orbit nearest the earth, and next the sun, in the second orbit above the earth; then came the morning star and the star sacred to Hermes, moving in orbits which have an equal swiftness with the sun, but in an opposite direction; and this is the reason why the sun and Hermes and Lucifer overtake and are overtaken by each other. To enumerate the places which he assigned to the other stars, and to give all the reasons why he assigned them, although a secondary matter, would give more trouble than the primary. These things at some future time, when we are at leisure, may have the consideration which they deserve, but not at present.

Now, when all the stars which were necessary to the creation of time had attained a motion suitable to them, and had become living creatures having bodies fastened by vital chains, and learnt their appointed task, moving in the motion of the diverse, which is diagonal, and passes through and is governed by the motion of the same, they revolved, some in a larger and some in a lesser orbit — those which had the lesser orbit revolving faster, and those which had the larger more slowly. Now by reason of the motion of the same, those which revolved fastest appeared to be overtaken by those which moved slower although they really overtook them; for the motion of the same made them all turn in a spiral, and, because some went one way and some another, that which receded most slowly from the sphere of the same, which was the swiftest, appeared to follow it most nearly. That there might be some visible measure of their relative swiftness and slowness as they proceeded in their eight courses, God lighted a fire, which we now call the sun, in the second from the earth of these orbits, that it might give light to the whole of heaven, and that the animals, as many as nature intended, might participate in number, learning arithmetic from the revolution of the same and the like. Thus then, and for this reason the night and the day were created, being the period of the one most intelligent revolution. And the month is accomplished when the moon has completed her orbit and overtaken the sun, and the year when the sun has completed his own orbit. Mankind, with hardly an exception, have not remarked the periods of the other stars, and they have no name for them, and do not measure them against one another by the help of number, and hence they can scarcely be said to know that their wanderings, being infinite in number and admirable for their variety, make up time. And yet there is no difficulty in seeing that the perfect number of time fulfils the perfect year when all the eight revolutions, having their relative degrees of swiftness, are accomplished together and attain their completion at the same time, measured by the rotation of the same and equally moving. After this manner, and for these reasons, came into being such of the stars as in their heavenly progress received reversals of motion, to the end that the created heaven might imitate the eternal nature, and be as like as possible to the perfect and intelligible animal.

Thus far and until the birth of time the created universe was made in the likeness of the original, but inasmuch as all animals were not yet comprehended therein, it was still unlike. What remained, the creator then proceeded to fashion after the nature of the pattern. Now as in the ideal animal the mind perceives ideas or species of a certain nature and number, he thought that this created animal ought to have species of a like nature and number. There are four such; one of them is the heavenly race of the gods; another, the race of birds whose way is in the air; the third, the watery species; and the fourth, the pedestrian and land creatures. Of the heavenly and divine, he created the greater part out of fire, that they might be the brightest of all things and fairest to behold, and he fashioned them after the likeness of the universe in the figure of a circle, and made them follow the intelligent motion of the supreme, distributing them over the whole circumference of heaven, which was to be a true cosmos or glorious world spangled with them all over. And he gave to each of them two movements: the first, a movement on the same spot after the same manner, whereby they ever continue to think consistently the same thoughts about the same things; the second, a forward movement, in which they are controlled by the revolution of the same and the like; but by the other five motions they were unaffected, in order that each of them might attain the highest perfection. And for this reason the fixed stars were created, to be divine and eternal animals, ever-abiding and revolving after the same manner and on the same spot; and the other stars which reverse their motion and are subject to deviations of this kind, were created in the manner already described. The earth, which is our nurse, clinging (or 'circling') around the pole which is extended through the universe, he framed to be the guardian and artificer of night and day, first and eldest of gods that are in the interior of heaven. Vain would be the attempt to tell all the figures of them circling as in dance, and their juxtapositions, and the return of them in their revolutions upon themselves, and their approximations, and to say which of these deities in their conjunctions meet, and which of them are in opposition, and in what order they get behind and before one another, and when they are severally eclipsed to our sight and again reappear, sending terrors and intimations of the future to those who cannot calculate their movements — to attempt to tell of all this without a visible representation of the heavenly system would be labour in vain. Enough on this head; and now let what we have said about the nature of the created and visible gods have an end.

To know or tell the origin of the other divinities is beyond us, and we must accept the traditions of the men of old time who affirm themselves to be the offspring of the gods — that is what they say — and they must surely have known their own ancestors. How can we doubt the word of the children of the gods? Although they give no probable or certain proofs, still, as they declare that they are speaking of what took place in their own family, we must conform to custom and believe them. In this manner, then, according to them, the genealogy of these gods is to be received and set forth.

Oceanus and Tethys were the children of Earth and Heaven, and from these sprang Phorcys and Cronos and Rhea, and all that generation; and from Cronos and Rhea sprang Zeus and Here, and all those who are said to be their brethren, and others who were the children of these.

Now, when all of them, both those who visibly appear in their revolutions as well as those other gods who are of a more retiring nature, had come into being, the creator of the universe addressed them in these words: 'Gods, children of gods, who are my works, and of whom I am the artificer and father, my creations are indissoluble, if so I will. All that is bound may be undone, but only an evil being would wish to undo that which is harmonious and happy. Wherefore, since ye are but creatures, ye are not altogether immortal and indissoluble, but ye shall certainly not be dissolved, nor be liable to the fate of death, having in my will a greater and mightier bond than those with which ye were bound at the time of your birth. And now listen to my instructions:— Three tribes of mortal beings remain to be created — without them the universe will be incomplete, for it will not contain every kind of animal which it ought to contain, if it is to be perfect. On the other hand, if they were created by me and received life at my hands, they would be on an equality with the gods. In order then that they may be mortal, and that this universe may be truly universal, do ye, according to your natures, betake yourselves to the formation of animals, imitating the power which was shown by me in creating you. The part of them worthy of the name immortal, which is called divine and is the guiding principle of those who are willing to follow justice and you — of that divine part I will myself sow the seed, and having made a beginning, I will hand the work over to you. And do ye then interweave the mortal with the immortal, and make and beget living creatures, and give them food, and make them to grow, and receive them again in death.'

Thus he spake, and once more into the cup in which he had previously mingled the soul of the universe he poured the remains of the elements, and mingled them in much the same manner; they were not, however, pure as before, but diluted to the second and third degree. And having made it he divided the whole mixture into souls equal in number to the stars, and assigned each soul to a star; and having there placed them as in a chariot, he showed them the nature of the universe, and declared to them the laws of destiny, according to which their first birth would be one and the same for all — no one should suffer a disadvantage at his hands; they were to be sown in the instruments of time severally adapted to them, and to come forth the most religious of animals; and as human nature was of two kinds, the superior race would hereafter be called man. Now, when they should be implanted in bodies by necessity, and be always gaining or losing some part of their bodily substance, then in the first place it would be necessary that they should all have in them one and the same faculty of sensation, arising out of irresistible impressions; in the second place, they must have love, in which pleasure and pain mingle; also fear and anger, and the feelings which are akin or opposite to them; if they conquered these they would live righteously, and if they were conquered by them, unrighteously. He who lived well during his appointed time was to return and dwell in his native star, and there he would have a blessed and congenial existence. But if he failed in attaining this, at the second birth he would pass into a woman, and if, when in that state of being, he did not desist from evil, he would continually be changed into some brute who resembled him in the evil nature which he had acquired, and would not cease from his toils and transformations until he followed the revolution of the same and the like within him, and overcame by the help of reason the turbulent and irrational mob of later accretions, made up of fire and air and water and earth, and returned to the form of his first and better state. Having given all these laws to his creatures, that he might be guiltless of future evil in any of them, the creator sowed some of them in the earth, and some in the moon, and some in the other instruments of time; and when he had sown them he committed to the younger gods the fashioning of their mortal bodies, and desired them to furnish what was still lacking to the human soul, and having made all the suitable additions, to rule over them, and to pilot the mortal animal in the best and wisest manner which they could, and avert from him all but self-inflicted evils.

When the creator had made all these ordinances he remained in his own accustomed nature, and his children heard and were obedient to their father's word, and receiving from him the immortal principle of a mortal creature, in imitation of their own creator they borrowed portions of fire, and earth, and water, and air from the world, which were hereafter to be restored — these they took and welded them together, not with the indissoluble chains by which they were themselves bound, but with little pegs too small to be visible, making up out of all the four elements each separate body, and fastening the courses of the immortal soul in a body which was in a state of perpetual influx and efflux. Now these courses, detained as in a vast river, neither overcame nor were overcome; but were hurrying and hurried to and fro, so that the whole animal was moved and progressed, irregularly however and irrationally and anyhow, in all the six directions of motion, wandering backwards and forwards, and right and left, and up and down, and in all the six directions. For great as was the advancing and retiring flood which provided nourishment, the affections produced by external contact caused still greater tumult — when the body of any one met and came into collision with some external fire, or with the solid earth or the gliding waters, or was caught in the tempest borne on the air, and the motions produced by any of these impulses were carried through the body to the soul. All such motions have consequently received the general name of 'sensations,' which they still retain. And they did in fact at that time create a very great and mighty movement; uniting with the ever-flowing stream in stirring up and violently shaking the courses of the soul, they completely stopped the revolution of the same by their opposing current, and hindered it from predominating and advancing; and they so disturbed the nature of the other or diverse, that the three double intervals (i.e. between 1, 2, 4, 8), and the three triple intervals (i.e. between 1, 3, 9, 27), together with the mean terms and connecting links which are expressed by the ratios of 3:2, and 4:3, and of 9:8 — these, although they cannot be wholly undone except by him who united them, were twisted by them in all sorts of ways, and the circles were broken and disordered in every possible manner, so that when they moved they were tumbling to pieces, and moved irrationally, at one time in a reverse direction, and then again obliquely, and then upside down, as you might imagine a person who is upside down and has his head leaning upon the ground and his feet up against something in the air; and when he is in such a position, both he and the spectator fancy that the right of either is his left, and the left right. If, when powerfully experiencing these and similar effects, the revolutions of the soul come in contact with some external thing, either of the class of the same or of the other, they speak of the same or of the other in a manner the very opposite of the truth; and they become false and foolish, and there is no course or revolution in them which has a guiding or directing power; and if again any sensations enter in violently from without and drag after them the whole vessel of the soul, then the courses of the soul, though they seem to conquer, are really conquered.

And by reason of all these affections, the soul, when encased in a mortal body, now, as in the beginning, is at first without intelligence; but when the flood of growth and nutriment abates, and the courses of the soul, calming down, go their own way and become steadier as time goes on, then the several circles return to their natural form, and their revolutions are corrected, and they call the same and the other by their right names, and make the possessor of them to become a rational being. And if these combine in him with any true nurture or education, he attains the fulness and health of the perfect man, and escapes the worst disease of all; but if he neglects education he walks lame to the end of his life, and returns imperfect and good for nothing to the world below. This, however, is a later stage; at present we must treat more exactly the subject before us, which involves a preliminary enquiry into the generation of the body and its members, and as to how the soul was created — for what reason and by what providence of the gods; and holding fast to probability, we must pursue our way.

First, then, the gods, imitating the spherical shape of the universe, enclosed the two divine courses in a spherical body, that, namely, which we now term the head, being the most divine part of us and the lord of all that is in us: to this the gods, when they put together the body, gave all the other members to be servants, considering that it partook of every sort of motion. In order then that it might not tumble about among the high and deep places of the earth, but might be able to get over the one and out of the other, they provided the body to be its vehicle and means of locomotion; which consequently had length and was furnished with four limbs extended and flexible; these God contrived to be instruments of locomotion with which it might take hold and find support, and so be able to pass through all places, carrying on high the dwelling-place of the most sacred and divine part of us. Such was the origin of legs and hands, which for this reason were attached to every man; and the gods, deeming the front part of man to be more honourable and more fit to command than the hinder part, made us to move mostly in a forward direction. Wherefore man must needs have his front part unlike and distinguished from the rest of his body.

And so in the vessel of the head, they first of all put a face in which they inserted organs to minister in all things to the providence of the soul, and they appointed this part, which has authority, to be by nature the part which is in front. And of the organs they first contrived the eyes to give light, and the principle according to which they were inserted was as follows: So much of fire as would not burn, but gave a gentle light, they formed into a substance akin to the light of every-day life; and the pure fire which is within us and related thereto they made to flow through the eyes in a stream smooth and dense, compressing the whole eye, and especially the centre part, so that it kept out everything of a coarser nature, and allowed to pass only this pure element. When the light of day surrounds the stream of vision, then like falls upon like, and they coalesce, and one body is formed by natural affinity in the line of vision, wherever the light that falls from within meets with an external object. And the whole stream of vision, being similarly affected in virtue of similarity, diffuses the motions of what it touches or what touches it over the whole body, until they reach the soul, causing that perception which we call sight. But when night comes on and the external and kindred fire departs, then the stream of vision is cut off; for going forth to an unlike element it is changed and extinguished, being no longer of one nature with the surrounding atmosphere which is now deprived of fire: and so the eye no longer sees, and we feel disposed to sleep. For when the eyelids, which the gods invented for the preservation of sight, are closed, they keep in the internal fire; and the power of the fire diffuses and equalizes the inward motions; when they are equalized, there is rest, and when the rest is profound, sleep comes over us scarce disturbed by dreams; but where the greater motions still remain, of whatever nature and in whatever locality, they engender corresponding visions in dreams, which are remembered by us when we are awake and in the external world. And now there is no longer any difficulty in understanding the creation of images in mirrors and all smooth and bright surfaces. For from the communion of the internal and external fires, and again from the union of them and their numerous transformations when they meet in the mirror, all these appearances of necessity arise, when the fire from the face coalesces with the fire from the eye on the bright and smooth surface. And right appears left and left right, because the visual rays come into contact with the rays emitted by the object in a manner contrary to the usual mode of meeting; but the right appears right, and the left left, when the position of one of the two concurring lights is reversed; and this happens when the mirror is concave and its smooth surface repels the right stream of vision to the left side, and the left to the right (He is speaking of two kinds of mirrors, first the plane, secondly the concave; and the latter is supposed to be placed, first horizontally, and then vertically.). Or if the mirror be turned vertically, then the concavity makes the countenance appear to be all upside down, and the lower rays are driven upwards and the upper downwards.

All these are to be reckoned among the second and co-operative causes which God, carrying into execution the idea of the best as far as possible, uses as his ministers. They are thought by most men not to be the second, but the prime causes of all things, because they freeze and heat, and contract and dilate, and the like. But they are not so, for they are incapable of reason or intellect; the only being which can properly have mind is the invisible soul, whereas fire and water, and earth and air, are all of them visible bodies. The lover of intellect and knowledge ought to explore causes of intelligent nature first of all, and, secondly, of those things which, being moved by others, are compelled to move others. And this is what we too must do. Both kinds of causes should be acknowledged by us, but a distinction should be made between those which are endowed with mind and are the workers of things fair and good, and those which are deprived of intelligence and always produce chance effects without order or design. Of the second or co-operative causes of sight, which help to give to the eyes the power which they now possess, enough has been said. I will therefore now proceed to speak of the higher use and purpose for which God has given them to us. The sight in my opinion is the source of the greatest benefit to us, for had we never seen the stars, and the sun, and the heaven, none of the words which we have spoken about the universe would ever have been uttered. But now the sight of day and night, and the months and the revolutions of the years, have created number, and have given us a conception of time, and the power of enquiring about the nature of the universe; and from this source we have derived philosophy, than which no greater good ever was or will be given by the gods to mortal man. This is the greatest boon of sight: and of the lesser benefits why should I speak? even the ordinary man if he were deprived of them would bewail his loss, but in vain. Thus much let me say however: God invented and gave us sight to the end that we might behold the courses of intelligence in the heaven, and apply them to the courses of our own intelligence which are akin to them, the unperturbed to the perturbed; and that we, learning them and partaking of the natural truth of reason, might imitate the absolutely unerring courses of God and regulate our own vagaries. The same may be affirmed of speech and hearing: they have been given by the gods to the same end and for a like reason. For this is the principal end of speech, whereto it most contributes. Moreover, so much of music as is adapted to the sound of the voice and to the sense of hearing is granted to us for the sake of harmony; and harmony, which has motions akin to the revolutions of our souls, is not regarded by the intelligent votary of the Muses as given by them with a view to irrational pleasure, which is deemed to be the purpose of it in our day, but as meant to correct any discord which may have arisen in the courses of the soul, and to be our ally in bringing her into harmony and agreement with herself; and rhythm too was given by them for the same reason, on account of the irregular and graceless ways which prevail among mankind generally, and to help us against them.

Thus far in what we have been saying, with small exception, the works of intelligence have been set forth; and now we must place by the side of them in our discourse the things which come into being through necessity — for the creation is mixed, being made up of necessity and mind. Mind, the ruling power, persuaded necessity to bring the greater part of created things to perfection, and thus and after this manner in the beginning, when the influence of reason got the better of necessity, the universe was created. But if a person will truly tell of the way in which the work was accomplished, he must include the other influence of the variable cause as well. Wherefore, we must return again and find another suitable beginning, as about the former matters, so also about these. To which end we must consider the nature of fire, and water, and air, and earth, such as they were prior to the creation of the heaven, and what was happening to them in this previous state; for no one has as yet explained the manner of their generation, but we speak of fire and the rest of them, whatever they mean, as though men knew their natures, and we maintain them to be the first principles and letters or elements of the whole, when they cannot reasonably be compared by a man of any sense even to syllables or first compounds. And let me say thus much: I will not now speak of the first principle or principles of all things, or by whatever name they are to be called, for this reason because it is difficult to set forth my opinion according to the method of discussion which we are at present employing. Do not imagine, any more than I can bring myself to imagine, that I should be right in undertaking so great and difficult a task. Remembering what I said at first about probability, I will do my best to give as probable an explanation as any other — or rather, more probable; and I will first go back to the beginning and try to speak of each thing and of all. Once more, then, at the commencement of my discourse, I call upon God, and beg him to be our saviour out of a strange and unwonted enquiry, and to bring us to the haven of probability. So now let us begin again.

This new beginning of our discussion of the universe requires a fuller division than the former; for then we made two classes, now a third must be revealed. The two sufficed for the former discussion: one, which we assumed, was a pattern intelligible and always the same; and the second was only the imitation of the pattern, generated and visible. There is also a third kind which we did not distinguish at the time, conceiving that the two would be enough. But now the argument seems to require that we should set forth in words another kind, which is difficult of explanation and dimly seen. What nature are we to attribute to this new kind of being? We reply, that it is the receptacle, and in a manner the nurse, of all generation. I have spoken the truth; but I must express myself in clearer language, and this will be an arduous task for many reasons, and in particular because I must first raise questions concerning fire and the other elements, and determine what each of them is; for to say, with any probability or certitude, which of them should be called water rather than fire, and which should be called any of them rather than all or some one of them, is a difficult matter. How, then, shall we settle this point, and what questions about the elements may be fairly raised?

In the first place, we see that what we just now called water, by condensation, I suppose, becomes stone and earth; and this same element, when melted and dispersed, passes into vapour and air. Air, again, when inflamed, becomes fire; and again fire, when condensed and extinguished, passes once more into the form of air; and once more, air, when collected and condensed, produces cloud and mist; and from these, when still more compressed, comes flowing water, and from water comes earth and stones once more; and thus generation appears to be transmitted from one to the other in a circle. Thus, then, as the several elements never present themselves in the same form, how can any one have the assurance to assert positively that any of them, whatever it may be, is one thing rather than another? No one can. But much the safest plan is to speak of them as follows:— Anything which we see to be continually changing, as, for example, fire, we must not call 'this' or 'that,' but rather say that it is 'of such a nature'; nor let us speak of water as 'this'; but always as 'such'; nor must we imply that there is any stability in any of those things which we indicate by the use of the words 'this' and 'that,' supposing ourselves to signify something thereby; for they are too volatile to be detained in any such expressions as 'this,' or 'that,' or 'relative to this,' or any other mode of speaking which represents them as permanent. We ought not to apply 'this' to any of them, but rather the word 'such'; which expresses the similar principle circulating in each and all of them; for example, that should be called 'fire' which is of such a nature always, and so of everything that has generation. That in which the elements severally grow up, and appear, and decay, is alone to be called by the name 'this' or 'that'; but that which is of a certain nature, hot or white, or anything which admits of opposite qualities, and all things that are compounded of them, ought not to be so denominated. Let me make another attempt to explain my meaning more clearly. Suppose a person to make all kinds of figures of gold and to be always transmuting one form into all the rest; — somebody points to one of them and asks what it is. By far the safest and truest answer is, That is gold; and not to call the triangle or any other figures which are formed in the gold 'these,' as though they had existence, since they are in process of change while he is making the assertion; but if the questioner be willing to take the safe and indefinite expression, 'such,' we should be satisfied. And the same argument applies to the universal nature which receives all bodies — that must be always called the same; for, while receiving all things, she never departs at all from her own nature, and never in any way, or at any time, assumes a form like that of any of the things which enter into her; she is the natural recipient of all impressions, and is stirred and informed by them, and appears different from time to time by reason of them. But the forms which enter into and go out of her are the likenesses of real existences modelled after their patterns in a wonderful and inexplicable manner, which we will hereafter investigate. For the present we have only to conceive of three natures: first, that which is in process of generation; secondly, that in which the generation takes place; and thirdly, that of which the thing generated is a resemblance. And we may liken the receiving principle to a mother, and the source or spring to a father, and the intermediate nature to a child; and may remark further, that if the model is to take every variety of form, then the matter in which the model is fashioned will not be duly prepared, unless it is formless, and free from the impress of any of those shapes which it is hereafter to receive from without. For if the matter were like any of the supervening forms, then whenever any opposite or entirely different nature was stamped upon its surface, it would take the impression badly, because it would intrude its own shape. Wherefore, that which is to receive all forms should have no form; as in making perfumes they first contrive that the liquid substance which is to receive the scent shall be as inodorous as possible; or as those who wish to impress figures on soft substances do not allow any previous impression to remain, but begin by making the surface as even and smooth as possible. In the same way that which is to receive perpetually and through its whole extent the resemblances of all eternal beings ought to be devoid of any particular form. Wherefore, the mother and receptacle of all created and visible and in any way sensible things, is not to be termed earth, or air, or fire, or water, or any of their compounds or any of the elements from which these are derived, but is an invisible and formless being which receives all things and in some mysterious way partakes of the intelligible, and is most incomprehensible. In saying this we shall not be far wrong; as far, however, as we can attain to a knowledge of her from the previous considerations, we may truly say that fire is that part of her nature which from time to time is inflamed, and water that which is moistened, and that the mother substance becomes earth and air, in so far as she receives the impressions of them.

Let us consider this question more precisely. Is there any self-existent fire? and do all those things which we call self-existent exist? or are only those things which we see, or in some way perceive through the bodily organs, truly existent, and nothing whatever besides them? And is all that which we call an intelligible essence nothing at all, and only a name? Here is a question which we must not leave unexamined or undetermined, nor must we affirm too confidently that there can be no decision; neither must we interpolate in our present long discourse a digression equally long, but if it is possible to set forth a great principle in a few words, that is just what we want.

Thus I state my view:— If mind and true opinion are two distinct classes, then I say that there certainly are these self-existent ideas unperceived by sense, and apprehended only by the mind; if, however, as some say, true opinion differs in no respect from mind, then everything that we perceive through the body is to be regarded as most real and certain. But we must affirm them to be distinct, for they have a distinct origin and are of a different nature; the one is implanted in us by instruction, the other by persuasion; the one is always accompanied by true reason, the other is without reason; the one cannot be overcome by persuasion, but the other can: and lastly, every man may be said to share in true opinion, but mind is the attribute of the gods and of very few men. Wherefore also we must acknowledge that there is one kind of being which is always the same, uncreated and indestructible, never receiving anything into itself from without, nor itself going out to any other, but invisible and imperceptible by any sense, and of which the contemplation is granted to intelligence only. And there is another nature of the same name with it, and like to it, perceived by sense, created, always in motion, becoming in place and again vanishing out of place, which is apprehended by opinion and sense. And there is a third nature, which is space, and is eternal, and admits not of destruction and provides a home for all created things, and is apprehended without the help of sense, by a kind of spurious reason, and is hardly real; which we beholding as in a dream, say of all existence that it must of necessity be in some place and occupy a space, but that what is neither in heaven nor in earth has no existence. Of these and other things of the same kind, relating to the true and waking reality of nature, we have only this dreamlike sense, and we are unable to cast off sleep and determine the truth about them. For an image, since the reality, after which it is modelled, does not belong to it, and it exists ever as the fleeting shadow of some other, must be inferred to be in another (i.e. in space), grasping existence in some way or other, or it could not be at all. But true and exact reason, vindicating the nature of true being, maintains that while two things (i.e. the image and space) are different they cannot exist one of them in the other and so be one and also two at the same time.

Thus have I concisely given the result of my thoughts; and my verdict is that being and space and generation, these three, existed in their three ways before the heaven; and that the nurse of generation, moistened by water and inflamed by fire, and receiving the forms of earth and air, and experiencing all the affections which accompany these, presented a strange variety of appearances; and being full of powers which were neither similar nor equally balanced, was never in any part in a state of equipoise, but swaying unevenly hither and thither, was shaken by them, and by its motion again shook them; and the elements when moved were separated and carried continually, some one way, some another; as, when grain is shaken and winnowed by fans and other instruments used in the threshing of corn, the close and heavy particles are borne away and settle in one direction, and the loose and light particles in another. In this manner, the four kinds or elements were then shaken by the receiving vessel, which, moving like a winnowing machine, scattered far away from one another the elements most unlike, and forced the most similar elements into close contact. Wherefore also the various elements had different places before they were arranged so as to form the universe. At first, they were all without reason and measure. But when the world began to get into order, fire and water and earth and air had only certain faint traces of themselves, and were altogether such as everything might be expected to be in the absence of God; this, I say, was their nature at that time, and God fashioned them by form and number. Let it be consistently maintained by us in all that we say that God made them as far as possible the fairest and best, out of things which were not fair and good. And now I will endeavour to show you the disposition and generation of them by an unaccustomed argument, which I am compelled to use; but I believe that you will be able to follow me, for your education has made you familiar with the methods of science.

In the first place, then, as is evident to all, fire and earth and water and air are bodies. And every sort of body possesses solidity, and every solid must necessarily be contained in planes; and every plane rectilinear figure is composed of triangles; and all triangles are originally of two kinds, both of which are made up of one right and two acute angles; one of them has at either end of the base the half of a divided right angle, having equal sides, while in the other the right angle is divided into unequal parts, having unequal sides. These, then, proceeding by a combination of probability with demonstration, we assume to be the original elements of fire and the other bodies; but the principles which are prior to these God only knows, and he of men who is the friend of God. And next we have to determine what are the four most beautiful bodies which are unlike one another, and of which some are capable of resolution into one another; for having discovered thus much, we shall know the true origin of earth and fire and of the proportionate and intermediate elements. And then we shall not be willing to allow that there are any distinct kinds of visible bodies fairer than these. Wherefore we must endeavour to construct the four forms of bodies which excel in beauty, and then we shall be able to say that we have sufficiently apprehended their nature. Now of the two triangles, the isosceles has one form only; the scalene or unequal-sided has an infinite number. Of the infinite forms we must select the most beautiful, if we are to proceed in due order, and any one who can point out a more beautiful form than ours for the construction of these bodies, shall carry off the palm, not as an enemy, but as a friend. Now, the one which we maintain to be the most beautiful of all the many triangles (and we need not speak of the others) is that of which the double forms a third triangle which is equilateral; the reason of this would be long to tell; he who disproves what we are saying, and shows that we are mistaken, may claim a friendly victory. Then let us choose two triangles, out of which fire and the other elements have been constructed, one isosceles, the other having the square of the longer side equal to three times the square of the lesser side.

Now is the time to explain what was before obscurely said: there was an error in imagining that all the four elements might be generated by and into one another; this, I say, was an erroneous supposition, for there are generated from the triangles which we have selected four kinds — three from the one which has the sides unequal; the fourth alone is framed out of the isosceles triangle. Hence they cannot all be resolved into one another, a great number of small bodies being combined into a few large ones, or the converse. But three of them can be thus resolved and compounded, for they all spring from one, and when the greater bodies are broken up, many small bodies will spring up out of them and take their own proper figures; or, again, when many small bodies are dissolved into their triangles, if they become one, they will form one large mass of another kind. So much for their passage into one another. I have now to speak of their several kinds, and show out of what combinations of numbers each of them was formed. The first will be the simplest and smallest construction, and its element is that triangle which has its hypotenuse twice the lesser side. When two such triangles are joined at the diagonal, and this is repeated three times, and the triangles rest their diagonals and shorter sides on the same point as a centre, a single equilateral triangle is formed out of six triangles; and four equilateral triangles, if put together, make out of every three plane angles one solid angle, being that which is nearest to the most obtuse of plane angles; and out of the combination of these four angles arises the first solid form which distributes into equal and similar parts the whole circle in which it is inscribed. The second species of solid is formed out of the same triangles, which unite as eight equilateral triangles and form one solid angle out of four plane angles, and out of six such angles the second body is completed. And the third body is made up of 120 triangular elements, forming twelve solid angles, each of them included in five plane equilateral triangles, having altogether twenty bases, each of which is an equilateral triangle. The one element (that is, the triangle which has its hypotenuse twice the lesser side) having generated these figures, generated no more; but the isosceles triangle produced the fourth elementary figure, which is compounded of four such triangles, joining their right angles in a centre, and forming one equilateral quadrangle. Six of these united form eight solid angles, each of which is made by the combination of three plane right angles; the figure of the body thus composed is a cube, having six plane quadrangular equilateral bases. There was yet a fifth combination which God used in the delineation of the universe.

Now, he who, duly reflecting on all this, enquires whether the worlds are to be regarded as indefinite or definite in number, will be of opinion that the notion of their indefiniteness is characteristic of a sadly indefinite and ignorant mind. He, however, who raises the question whether they are to be truly regarded as one or five, takes up a more reasonable position. Arguing from probabilities, I am of opinion that they are one; another, regarding the question from another point of view, will be of another mind. But, leaving this enquiry, let us proceed to distribute the elementary forms, which have now been created in idea, among the four elements.

To earth, then, let us assign the cubical form; for earth is the most immoveable of the four and the most plastic of all bodies, and that which has the most stable bases must of necessity be of such a nature. Now, of the triangles which we assumed at first, that which has two equal sides is by nature more firmly based than that which has unequal sides; and of the compound figures which are formed out of either, the plane equilateral quadrangle has necessarily a more stable basis than the equilateral triangle, both in the whole and in the parts. Wherefore, in assigning this figure to earth, we adhere to probability; and to water we assign that one of the remaining forms which is the least moveable; and the most moveable of them to fire; and to air that which is intermediate. Also we assign the smallest body to fire, and the greatest to water, and the intermediate in size to air; and, again, the acutest body to fire, and the next in acuteness to air, and the third to water. Of all these elements, that which has the fewest bases must necessarily be the most moveable, for it must be the acutest and most penetrating in every way, and also the lightest as being composed of the smallest number of similar particles: and the second body has similar properties in a second degree, and the third body in the third degree. Let it be agreed, then, both according to strict reason and according to probability, that the pyramid is the solid which is the original element and seed of fire; and let us assign the element which was next in the order of generation to air, and the third to water. We must imagine all these to be so small that no single particle of any of the four kinds is seen by us on account of their smallness: but when many of them are collected together their aggregates are seen. And the ratios of their numbers, motions, and other properties, everywhere God, as far as necessity allowed or gave consent, has exactly perfected, and harmonized in due proportion.

>From all that we have just been saying about the elements or kinds, the most probable conclusion is as follows:— earth, when meeting with fire and dissolved by its sharpness, whether the dissolution take place in the fire itself or perhaps in some mass of air or water, is borne hither and thither, until its parts, meeting together and mutually harmonising, again become earth; for they can never take any other form. But water, when divided by fire or by air, on re-forming, may become one part fire and two parts air; and a single volume of air divided becomes two of fire. Again, when a small body of fire is contained in a larger body of air or water or earth, and both are moving, and the fire struggling is overcome and broken up, then two volumes of fire form one volume of air; and when air is overcome and cut up into small pieces, two and a half parts of air are condensed into one part of water. Let us consider the matter in another way. When one of the other elements is fastened upon by fire, and is cut by the sharpness of its angles and sides, it coalesces with the fire, and then ceases to be cut by them any longer. For no element which is one and the same with itself can be changed by or change another of the same kind and in the same state. But so long as in the process of transition the weaker is fighting against the stronger, the dissolution continues. Again, when a few small particles, enclosed in many larger ones, are in process of decomposition and extinction, they only cease from their tendency to extinction when they consent to pass into the conquering nature, and fire becomes air and air water. But if bodies of another kind go and attack them (i.e. the small particles), the latter continue to be dissolved until, being completely forced back and dispersed, they make their escape to their own kindred, or else, being overcome and assimilated to the conquering power, they remain where they are and dwell with their victors, and from being many

become one. And owing to these affections, all things are changing their place, for by the motion of the receiving vessel the bulk of each class is distributed into its proper place; but those things which become unlike themselves and like other things, are hurried by the shaking into the place of the things to which they grow like.

Now all unmixed and primary bodies are produced by such causes as these. As to the subordinate species which are included in the greater kinds, they are to be attributed to the varieties in the structure of the two original triangles. For either structure did not originally produce the triangle of one size only, but some larger and some smaller, and there are as many sizes as there are species of the four elements. Hence when they are mingled with themselves and with one another there is an endless variety of them, which those who would arrive at the probable truth of nature ought duly to consider.

Unless a person comes to an understanding about the nature and conditions of rest and motion, he will meet with many difficulties in the discussion which follows. Something has been said of this matter already, and something more remains to be said, which is, that motion never exists in what is uniform. For to conceive that anything can be moved without a mover is hard or indeed impossible, and equally impossible to conceive that there can be a mover unless there be something which can be moved — motion cannot exist where either of these are wanting, and for these to be uniform is impossible; wherefore we must assign rest to uniformity and motion to the want of uniformity. Now inequality is the cause of the nature which is wanting in uniformity; and of this we have already described the origin. But there still remains the further point — why things when divided after their kinds do not cease to pass through one another and to change their place — which we will now proceed to explain. In the revolution of the universe are comprehended all the four elements, and this being circular and having a tendency to come together, compresses everything and will not allow any place to be left void. Wherefore, also, fire above all things penetrates everywhere, and air next, as being next in rarity of the elements; and the two other elements in like manner penetrate according to their degrees of rarity. For those things which are composed of the largest particles have the largest void left in their compositions, and those which are composed of the smallest particles have the least. And the contraction caused by the compression thrusts the smaller particles into the interstices of the larger. And thus, when the small parts are placed side by side with the larger, and the lesser divide the greater and the greater unite the lesser, all the elements are borne up and down and hither and thither towards their own places; for the change in the size of each changes its position in space. And these causes generate an inequality which is always maintained, and is continually creating a perpetual motion of the elements in all time.

In the next place we have to consider that there are divers kinds of fire. There are, for example, first, flame; and secondly, those emanations of flame which do not burn but only give light to the eyes; thirdly, the remains of fire, which are seen in red-hot embers after the flame has been extinguished. There are similar differences in the air; of which the brightest part is called the aether, and the most turbid sort mist and darkness; and there are various other nameless kinds which arise from the inequality of the triangles. Water, again, admits in the first place of a division into two kinds; the one liquid and the other fusile. The liquid kind is composed of the small and unequal particles of water; and moves itself and is moved by other bodies owing to the want of uniformity and the shape of its particles; whereas the fusile kind, being formed of large and uniform particles, is more stable than the other, and is heavy and compact by reason of its uniformity. But when fire gets in and dissolves the particles and destroys the uniformity, it has greater mobility, and becoming fluid is thrust forth by the neighbouring air and spreads upon the earth; and this dissolution of the solid masses is called melting, and their spreading out upon the earth flowing. Again, when the fire goes out of the fusile substance, it does not pass into a vacuum, but into the neighbouring air; and the air which is displaced forces together the liquid and still moveable mass into the place which was occupied by the fire, and unites it with itself. Thus compressed the mass resumes its equability, and is again at unity with itself, because the fire which was the author of the inequality has retreated; and this departure of the fire is called cooling, and the coming together which follows upon it is termed congealment. Of all the kinds termed fusile, that which is the densest and is formed out of the finest and most uniform parts is that most precious possession called gold, which is hardened by filtration through rock; this is unique in kind, and has both a glittering and a yellow colour. A shoot of gold, which is so dense as to be very hard, and takes a black colour, is termed adamant. There is also another kind which has parts nearly like gold, and of which there are several species; it is denser than gold, and it contains a small and fine portion of earth, and is therefore harder, yet also lighter because of the great interstices which it has within itself; and this substance, which is one of the bright and denser kinds of water, when solidified is called copper. There is an alloy of earth mingled with it, which, when the two parts grow old and are disunited, shows itself separately and is called rust. The remaining phenomena of the same kind there will be no difficulty in reasoning out by the method of probabilities. A man may sometimes set aside meditations about eternal things, and for recreation turn to consider the truths of generation which are probable only; he will thus gain a pleasure not to be repented of, and secure for himself while he lives a wise and moderate pastime. Let us grant ourselves this indulgence, and go through the probabilities relating to the same subjects which follow next in order.

Water which is mingled with fire, so much as is fine and liquid (being so called by reason of its motion and the way in which it rolls along the ground), and soft, because its bases give way and are less stable than those of earth, when separated from fire and air and isolated, becomes more uniform, and by their retirement is compressed into itself; and if the condensation be very great, the water above the earth becomes hail, but on the earth, ice; and that which is congealed in a less degree and is only half solid, when above the earth is called snow, and when upon the earth, and condensed from dew, hoar-frost. Then, again, there are the numerous kinds of water which have been mingled with one another, and are distilled through plants which grow in the earth; and this whole class is called by the name of juices or saps. The unequal admixture of these fluids creates a variety of species; most of them are nameless, but four which are of a fiery nature are clearly distinguished and have names. First, there is wine, which warms the soul as well as the body: secondly, there is the oily nature, which is smooth and divides the visual ray, and for this reason is bright and shining and of a glistening appearance, including pitch, the juice of the castor berry, oil itself, and other things of a like kind: thirdly, there is the class of substances which expand the contracted parts of the mouth, until they return to their natural state, and by reason of this property create sweetness; — these are included under the general name of honey: and, lastly, there is a frothy nature, which differs from all juices, having a burning quality which dissolves the flesh; it is called opos (a vegetable acid).

As to the kinds of earth, that which is filtered through water passes into stone in the following manner:— The water which mixes with the earth and is broken up in the process changes into air, and taking this form mounts into its own place. But as there is no surrounding vacuum it thrusts away the neighbouring air, and this being rendered heavy, and, when it is displaced, having been poured around the mass of earth, forcibly compresses it and drives it into the vacant space whence the new air had come up; and the earth when compressed by the air into an indissoluble union with water becomes rock. The fairer sort is that which is made up of equal and similar parts and is transparent; that which has the opposite qualities is inferior. But when all the watery part is suddenly drawn out by fire, a more brittle substance is formed, to which we give the name of pottery. Sometimes also moisture may remain, and the earth which has been fused by fire becomes, when cool, a certain stone of a black colour. A like separation of the water which had been copiously mingled with them may occur in two substances composed of finer particles of earth and of a briny nature; out of either of them a half-solid-body is then formed, soluble in water — the one, soda, which is used for purging away oil and earth, the other, salt, which harmonizes so well in combinations pleasing to the palate, and is, as the law testifies, a substance dear to the gods. The compounds of earth and water are not soluble by water, but by fire only, and for this reason:— Neither fire nor air melt masses of earth; for their particles, being smaller than the interstices in its structure, have plenty of room to move without forcing their way, and so they leave the earth unmelted and undissolved;

but particles of water, which are larger, force a passage, and dissolve and melt the earth. Wherefore earth when not consolidated by force is dissolved by water only; when consolidated, by nothing but fire; for this is the only body which can find an entrance. The cohesion of water again, when very strong, is dissolved by fire only — when weaker, then either by air or fire — the former entering the interstices, and the latter penetrating even the triangles. But nothing can dissolve air, when strongly condensed, which does not reach the elements or triangles; or if not strongly condensed, then only fire can dissolve it. As to bodies composed of earth and water, while the water occupies the vacant interstices of the earth in them which are compressed by force, the particles of water which approach them from without, finding no entrance, flow around the entire mass and leave it undissolved; but the particles of fire, entering into the interstices of the water, do to the water what water does to earth and fire to air (The text seems to be corrupt.), and are the sole causes of the compound body of earth and water liquefying and becoming fluid. Now these bodies are of two kinds; some of them, such as glass and the fusible sort of stones, have less water than they have earth; on the other hand, substances of the nature of wax and incense have more of water entering into their composition.

I have thus shown the various classes of bodies as they are diversified by their forms and combinations and changes into one another, and now I must endeavour to set forth their affections and the causes of them. In the first place, the bodies which I have been describing are necessarily objects of sense. But we have not yet considered the origin of flesh, or what belongs to flesh, or of that part of the soul which is mortal. And these things cannot be adequately explained without also explaining the affections which are concerned with sensation, nor the latter without the former: and yet to explain them together is hardly possible; for which reason we must assume first one or the other and afterwards examine the nature of our hypothesis. In order, then, that the affections may follow regularly after the elements, let us presuppose the existence of body and soul.

First, let us enquire what we mean by saying that fire is hot; and about this we may reason from the dividing or cutting power which it exercises on our bodies. We all of us feel that fire is sharp; and we may further consider the fineness of the sides, and the sharpness of the angles, and the smallness of the particles, and the swiftness of the motion — all this makes the action of fire violent and sharp, so that it cuts whatever it meets. And we must not forget that the original figure of fire (i.e. the pyramid), more than any other form, has a dividing power which cuts our bodies into small pieces (Kepmatizei), and thus naturally produces that affection which we call heat; and hence the origin of the name (thepmos, Kepma). Now, the opposite of this is sufficiently manifest; nevertheless we will not fail to describe it. For the larger particles of moisture which surround the body, entering in and driving out the lesser, but not being able to take their places, compress the moist principle in us; and this from being unequal and disturbed, is forced by them into a state of rest, which is due to equability and compression. But things which are contracted contrary to nature are by nature at war, and force themselves apart; and to this war and convulsion the name of shivering and trembling is given; and the whole affection and the cause of the affection are both termed cold. That is called hard to which our flesh yields, and soft which yields to our flesh; and things are also termed hard and soft relatively to one another. That which yields has a small base; but that which rests on quadrangular bases is firmly posed and belongs to the class which offers the greatest resistance; so too does that which is the most compact and therefore most repellent. The nature of the light and the heavy will be best understood when examined in connexion with our notions of above and below; for it is quite a mistake to suppose that the universe is parted into two regions, separate from and opposite to each other, the one a lower to which all things tend which have any bulk, and an upper to which things only ascend against their will. For as the universe is in the form of a sphere, all the extremities, being equidistant from the centre, are equally extremities, and the centre, which is equidistant from them, is equally to be regarded as the opposite of them all. Such being the nature of the world, when a person says that any of these points is above or below, may he not be justly charged with using an improper expression? For the centre of the world cannot be rightly called either above or below, but is the centre and nothing else; and the circumference is not the centre, and has in no one part of itself a different relation to the centre from what it has in any of the opposite parts. Indeed, when it is in every direction similar, how can one rightly give to it names which imply opposition? For if there were any solid body in equipoise at the centre of the universe, there would be nothing to draw it to this extreme rather than to that, for they are all perfectly similar; and if a person were to go round the world in a circle, he would often, when standing at the antipodes of his former position, speak of the same point as above and below; for, as I was saying just now, to speak of the whole which is in the form of a globe as having one part above and another below is not like a sensible man. The reason why these names are used, and the circumstances under which they are ordinarily applied by us to the division of the heavens, may be elucidated by the following supposition:— if a person were to stand in that part of the universe which is the appointed place of fire, and where there is the great mass of fire to which fiery bodies gather — if, I say, he were to ascend thither, and, having the power to do this, were to abstract particles of fire and put them in scales and weigh them, and then, raising the balance, were to draw the fire by force towards the uncongenial element of the air, it would be very evident that he could compel the smaller mass more readily than the larger; for when two things are simultaneously raised by one and the same power, the smaller body must necessarily yield to the superior power with less reluctance than the larger; and the larger body is called heavy and said to tend downwards, and the smaller body is called light and said to tend upwards. And we may detect ourselves who are upon the earth doing precisely the same thing. For we often separate earthy natures, and sometimes earth itself, and draw them into the uncongenial element of air by force and contrary to nature, both clinging to their kindred elements. But that which is smaller yields to the impulse given by us towards the dissimilar element more easily than the larger; and so we call the former light, and the place towards which it is impelled we call above, and the contrary state and place we call heavy and below respectively. Now the relations of these must necessarily vary, because the principal masses of the different elements hold opposite positions; for that which is light, heavy, below or above in one place will be found to be and become contrary and transverse and every way diverse in relation to that which is light, heavy, below or above in an opposite place. And about all of them this has to be considered:— that the tendency of each towards its kindred element makes the body which is moved heavy, and the place towards which the motion tends below, but things which have an opposite tendency we call by an opposite name. Such are the causes which we assign to these phenomena. As to the smooth and the rough, any one who sees them can explain the reason of them to another. For roughness is hardness mingled with irregularity, and smoothness is produced by the joint effect of uniformity and density.

The most important of the affections which concern the whole body remains to be considered — that is, the cause of pleasure and pain in the perceptions of which I have been speaking, and in all other things which are perceived by sense through the parts of the body, and have both pains and pleasures attendant on them. Let us imagine the causes of every affection, whether of sense or not, to be of the following nature, remembering that we have already distinguished between the nature which is easy and which is hard to move; for this is the direction in which we must hunt the prey which we mean to take. A body which is of a nature to be easily moved, on receiving an impression however slight, spreads abroad the motion in a circle, the parts communicating with each other, until at last, reaching the principle of mind, they announce the quality of the agent. But a body of the opposite kind, being immobile, and not extending to the surrounding region, merely receives the impression, and does not stir any of the neighbouring parts; and since the parts do not distribute the original impression to other parts, it has no effect of motion on the whole animal, and therefore produces no effect on the patient. This is true of the bones and hair and other more earthy parts of the human body; whereas what was said above relates mainly to sight and hearing, because they have in them the greatest amount of fire and air. Now we must conceive of pleasure and pain in this way. An impression produced in us contrary to nature and violent, if sudden, is painful; and, again, the sudden return to nature is pleasant; but a gentle and gradual return is imperceptible and vice versa. On the other hand the impression of sense which is most easily produced is most readily felt, but is not accompanied by pleasure or pain; such, for example, are the affections of the sight, which, as we said above, is a body naturally uniting with our body in the day-time; for cuttings and burnings and other affections which happen to the sight do not give pain, nor is there pleasure when the sight returns to its natural state; but the sensations are clearest and strongest according to the manner in which the eye is affected by the object, and itself strikes and touches it; there is no violence either in the contraction or dilation of the eye. But bodies formed of larger particles yield to the agent only with a struggle; and then they impart their motions to the whole and cause pleasure and pain — pain when alienated from their natural conditions, and pleasure when restored to them. Things which experience gradual withdrawings and emptyings of their nature, and great and sudden replenishments, fail to perceive the emptying, but are sensible of the replenishment; and so they occasion no pain, but the greatest pleasure, to the mortal part of the soul, as is manifest in the case of perfumes. But things which are changed all of a sudden, and only gradually and with difficulty return to their own nature, have effects in every way opposite to the former, as is evident in the case of burnings and cuttings of the body.

Thus have we discussed the general affections of the whole body, and the names of the agents which produce them. And now I will endeavour to speak of the affections of particular parts, and the causes and agents of them, as far as I am able. In the first place let us set forth what was omitted when we were speaking of juices, concerning the affections peculiar to the tongue. These too, like most of the other affections, appear to be caused by certain contractions and dilations, but they have besides more of roughness and smoothness than is found in other affections; for whenever earthy particles enter into the small veins which are the testing instruments of the tongue, reaching to the heart, and fall upon the moist, delicate portions of flesh — when, as they are dissolved, they contract and dry up the little veins, they are astringent if they are rougher, but if not so rough, then only harsh. Those of them which are of an abstergent nature, and purge the whole surface of the tongue, if they do it in excess, and so encroach as to consume some part of the flesh itself, like potash and soda, are all termed bitter. But the particles which are deficient in the alkaline quality, and which cleanse only moderately, are called salt, and having no bitterness or roughness, are regarded as rather agreeable than otherwise. Bodies which share in and are made smooth by the heat of the mouth, and which are inflamed, and again in turn inflame that which heats them, and which are so light that they are carried upwards to the sensations of the head, and cut all that comes in their way, by reason of these qualities in them, are all termed pungent. But when these same particles, refined by putrefaction, enter into the narrow veins, and are duly proportioned to the particles of earth and air which are there, they set them whirling about one another, and while they are in a whirl cause them to dash against and enter into one another, and so form hollows surrounding the particles that enter — which watery vessels of air (for a film of moisture, sometimes earthy, sometimes pure, is spread around the air) are hollow spheres of water; and those of them which are pure, are transparent, and are called bubbles, while those composed of the earthy liquid, which is in a state of general agitation and effervescence, are said to boil or ferment — of all these affections the cause is termed acid. And there is the opposite affection arising from an opposite cause, when the mass of entering particles, immersed in the moisture of the mouth, is congenial to the tongue, and smooths and oils over the roughness, and relaxes the parts which are unnaturally contracted, and contracts the parts which are relaxed, and disposes them all according to their nature; — that sort of remedy of violent affections is pleasant and agreeable to every man, and has the name sweet. But enough of this.

The faculty of smell does not admit of differences of kind; for all smells are of a half-formed nature, and no element is so proportioned as to have any smell. The veins about the nose are too narrow to admit earth and water, and too wide to detain fire and air; and for this reason no one ever perceives the smell of any of them; but smells always proceed from bodies that are damp, or putrefying, or liquefying, or evaporating, and are perceptible only in the intermediate state, when water is changing into air and air into water; and all of them are either vapour or mist. That which is passing out of air into water is mist, and that which is passing from water into air is vapour; and hence all smells are thinner than water and thicker than air. The proof of this is, that when there is any obstruction to the respiration, and a man draws in his breath by force, then no smell filters through, but the air without the smell alone penetrates. Wherefore the varieties of smell have no name, and they have not many, or definite and simple kinds; but they are distinguished only as painful and pleasant, the one sort irritating and disturbing the whole cavity which is situated between the head and the navel, the other having a soothing influence, and restoring this same region to an agreeable and natural condition.

In considering the third kind of sense, hearing, we must speak of the causes in which it originates. We may in general assume sound to be a blow which passes through the ears, and is transmitted by means of the air, the brain, and the blood, to the soul, and that hearing is the vibration of this blow, which begins in the head and ends in the region of the liver. The sound which moves swiftly is acute, and the sound which moves slowly is grave, and that which is regular is equable and smooth, and the reverse is harsh. A great body of sound is loud, and a small body of sound the reverse. Respecting the harmonies of sound I must hereafter speak.

There is a fourth class of sensible things, having many intricate varieties, which must now be distinguished. They are called by the general name of colours, and are a flame which emanates from every sort of body, and has particles corresponding to the sense of sight. I have spoken already, in what has preceded, of the causes which generate sight, and in this place it will be natural and suitable to give a rational theory of colours.

Of the particles coming from other bodies which fall upon the sight, some are smaller and some are larger, and some are equal to the parts of the sight itself. Those which are equal are imperceptible, and we call them transparent. The larger produce contraction, the smaller dilation, in the sight, exercising a power akin to that of hot and cold bodies on the flesh, or of astringent bodies on the tongue, or of those heating bodies which we termed pungent. White and black are similar effects of contraction and dilation in another sphere, and for this reason have a different appearance. Wherefore, we ought to term white that which dilates the visual ray, and the opposite of this is black. There is also a swifter motion of a different sort of fire which strikes and dilates the ray of sight until it reaches the eyes, forcing a way through their passages and melting them, and eliciting from them a union of fire and water which we call tears, being itself an opposite fire which comes to them from an opposite direction — the inner fire flashes forth like lightning, and the outer finds a way in and is extinguished in the moisture, and all sorts of colours are generated by the mixture. This affection is termed dazzling, and the object which produces it is called bright and flashing. There is another sort of fire which is intermediate, and which reaches and mingles with the moisture of the eye without flashing; and in this, the fire mingling with the ray of the moisture, produces a colour like blood, to which we give the name of red. A bright hue mingled with red and white gives the colour called auburn (Greek). The law of proportion, however, according to which the several colours are formed, even if a man knew he would be foolish in telling, for he could not give any necessary reason, nor indeed any tolerable or probable explanation of them. Again, red, when mingled with black and white, becomes purple, but it becomes umber (Greek) when the colours are burnt as well as mingled and the black is more thoroughly mixed with them. Flame-colour (Greek) is produced by a union of auburn and dun (Greek), and dun by an admixture of black and white; pale yellow (Greek), by an admixture of white and auburn. White and bright meeting, and falling upon a full black, become dark blue (Greek), and when dark blue mingles with white, a light blue (Greek) colour is formed, as flame-colour with black makes leek green (Greek). There will be no difficulty in seeing how and by what mixtures the colours derived from these are made according to the rules of probability. He, however, who should attempt to verify all this by experiment, would forget the difference of the human and divine nature. For God only has the knowledge and also the power which are able to combine many things into one and again resolve the one into many. But no man either is or ever will be able to accomplish either the one or the other operation.

These are the elements, thus of necessity then subsisting, which the creator of the fairest and best of created things associated with himself, when he made the self-sufficing and most perfect God, using the necessary causes as his ministers in the accomplishment of his work, but himself contriving the good in all his creations. Wherefore we may distinguish two sorts of causes, the one divine and the other necessary, and may seek for the divine in all things, as far as our nature admits, with a view to the blessed life; but the necessary kind only for the sake of the divine, considering that without them and when isolated from them, these higher things for which we look cannot be apprehended or received or in any way shared by us.

Seeing, then, that we have now prepared for our use the various classes of causes which are the material out of which the remainder of our discourse must be woven, just as wood is the material of the carpenter, let us revert in a few words to the point at which we began, and then endeavour to add on a suitable ending to the beginning of our tale.

As I said at first, when all things were in disorder God created in each thing in relation to itself, and in all things in relation to each other, all the measures and harmonies which they could possibly receive. For in those days nothing had any proportion except by accident; nor did any of the things which now have names deserve to be named at all — as, for example, fire, water, and the rest of the elements. All these the creator first set in order, and out of them he constructed the universe, which was a single animal comprehending in itself all other animals, mortal and immortal. Now of the divine, he himself was the creator, but the creation of the mortal he committed to his offspring. And they, imitating him, received from him the immortal principle of the soul; and around this they proceeded to fashion a mortal body, and made it to be the vehicle of the soul, and constructed within the body a soul of another nature which was mortal, subject to terrible and irresistible affections — first of all, pleasure, the greatest incitement to evil; then, pain, which deters from good; also rashness and fear, two foolish counsellors, anger hard to be appeased, and hope easily led astray; — these they mingled with irrational sense and with all-daring love according to necessary laws, and so framed man. Wherefore, fearing to pollute the divine any more than was absolutely unavoidable, they gave to the mortal nature a separate habitation in another part of the body, placing the neck between them to be the isthmus and boundary, which they constructed between the head and breast, to keep them apart. And in the breast, and in what is termed the thorax, they encased the mortal soul; and as the one part of this was superior and the other inferior they divided the cavity of the thorax into two parts, as the women's and men's apartments are divided in houses, and placed the midriff to be a wall of partition between them. That part of the inferior soul which is endowed with courage and passion and loves contention they settled nearer the head, midway between the midriff and the neck, in order that it might be under the rule of reason and might join with it in controlling and restraining the desires when they are no longer willing of their own accord to obey the word of command issuing from the citadel.

The heart, the knot of the veins and the fountain of the blood which races through all the limbs, was set in the place of guard, that when the might of passion was roused by reason making proclamation of any wrong assailing them from without or being perpetrated by the desires within, quickly the whole power of feeling in the body, perceiving these commands and threats, might obey and follow through every turn and alley, and thus allow the principle of the best to have the command in all of them. But the gods, foreknowing that the palpitation of the heart in the expectation of danger and the swelling and excitement of passion was caused by fire, formed and implanted as a supporter to the heart the lung, which was, in the first place, soft and bloodless, and also had within hollows like the pores of a sponge, in order that by receiving the breath and the drink, it might give coolness and the power of respiration and alleviate the heat. Wherefore they cut the air-channels leading to the lung, and placed the lung about the heart as a soft spring, that, when passion was rife within, the heart, beating against a yielding body, might be cooled and suffer less, and might thus become more ready to join with passion in the service of reason.

The part of the soul which desires meats and drinks and the other things of which it has need by reason of the bodily nature, they placed between the midriff and the boundary of the navel, contriving in all this region a sort of manger for the food of the body; and there they bound it down like a wild animal which was chained up with man, and must be nourished if man was to exist. They appointed this lower creation his place here in order that he might be always feeding at the manger, and have his dwelling as far as might be from the council-chamber, making as little noise and disturbance as possible, and permitting the best part to advise quietly for the good of the whole. And knowing that this lower principle in man would not comprehend reason, and even if attaining to some degree of perception would never naturally care for rational notions, but that it would be led away by phantoms and visions night and day — to be a remedy for this, God combined with it the liver, and placed it in the house of the lower nature, contriving that it should be solid and smooth, and bright and sweet, and should also have a bitter quality, in order that the power of thought, which proceeds from the mind, might be reflected as in a mirror which receives likenesses of objects and gives back images of them to the sight; and so might strike terror into the desires, when, making use of the bitter part of the liver, to which it is akin, it comes threatening and invading, and diffusing this bitter element swiftly through the whole liver produces colours like bile, and contracting every part makes it wrinkled and rough; and twisting out of its right place and contorting the lobe and closing and shutting up the vessels and gates, causes pain and loathing. And the converse happens when some gentle inspiration of the understanding pictures images of an opposite character, and allays the bile and bitterness by refusing to stir or touch the nature opposed to itself, but by making use of the natural sweetness of the liver, corrects all things and makes them to be right and smooth and free, and renders the portion of the soul which resides about the liver happy and joyful, enabling it to pass the night in peace, and to practise divination in sleep, inasmuch as it has no share in mind and reason. For the authors of our being, remembering the command of their father when he bade them create the human race as good as they could, that they might correct our inferior parts and make them to attain a measure of truth, placed in the liver the seat of divination. And herein is a proof that God has given the art of divination not to the wisdom, but to the foolishness of man. No man, when in his wits, attains prophetic truth and inspiration; but when he receives the inspired word, either his intelligence is enthralled in sleep, or he is demented by some distemper or possession. And he who would understand what he remembers to have been said, whether in a dream or when he was awake, by the prophetic and inspired nature, or would determine by reason the meaning of the apparitions which he has seen, and what indications they afford to this man or that, of past, present or future good and evil, must first recover his wits. But, while he continues demented, he cannot judge of the visions which he sees or the words which he utters; the ancient saying is very true, that 'only a man who has his wits can act or judge about himself and his own affairs.' And for this reason it is customary to appoint interpreters to be judges of the true inspiration. Some persons call them prophets; they are quite unaware that they are only the expositors of dark sayings and visions, and are not to be called prophets at all, but only interpreters of prophecy.

Such is the nature of the liver, which is placed as we have described in order that it may give prophetic intimations. During the life of each individual these intimations are plainer, but after his death the liver becomes blind, and delivers oracles too obscure to be intelligible. The neighbouring organ (the spleen) is situated on the left-hand side, and is constructed with a view of keeping the liver bright and pure — like a napkin, always ready prepared and at hand to clean the mirror. And hence, when any impurities arise in the region of the liver by reason of disorders of the body, the loose nature of the spleen, which is composed of a hollow and bloodless tissue, receives them all and clears them away, and when filled with the unclean matter, swells and festers, but, again, when the body is purged, settles down into the same place as before, and is humbled.

Concerning the soul, as to which part is mortal and which divine, and how and why they are separated, and where located, if God acknowledges that we have spoken the truth, then, and then only, can we be confident; still, we may venture to assert that what has been said by us is probable, and will be rendered more probable by investigation. Let us assume thus much.

The creation of the rest of the body follows next in order, and this we may investigate in a similar manner. And it appears to be very meet that the body should be framed on the following principles:—

The authors of our race were aware that we should be intemperate in eating and drinking, and take a good deal more than was necessary or proper, by reason of gluttony. In order then that disease might not quickly destroy us, and lest our mortal race should perish without fulfilling its end — intending to provide against this, the gods made what is called the lower belly, to be a receptacle for the superfluous meat and drink, and formed the convolution of the bowels, so that the food might be prevented from passing quickly through and compelling the body to require more food, thus producing insatiable gluttony, and making the whole race an enemy to philosophy and music, and rebellious against the divinest element within us.

The bones and flesh, and other similar parts of us, were made as follows. The first principle of all of them was the generation of the marrow. For the bonds of life which unite the soul with the body are made fast there, and they are the root and foundation of the human race. The marrow itself is created out of other materials: God took such of the primary triangles as were straight and smooth, and were adapted by their perfection to produce fire and water, and air and earth — these, I say, he separated from their kinds, and mingling them in due proportions with one another, made the marrow out of them to be a universal seed of the whole race of mankind; and in this seed he then planted and enclosed the souls, and in the original distribution gave to the marrow as many and various forms as the different kinds of souls were hereafter to receive. That which, like a field, was to receive the divine seed, he made round every way, and called that portion of the marrow, brain, intending that, when an animal was perfected, the vessel containing this substance should be the head; but that which was intended to contain the remaining and mortal part of the soul he distributed into figures at once round and elongated, and he called them all by the name 'marrow'; and to these, as to anchors, fastening the bonds of the whole soul, he proceeded to fashion around them the entire framework of our body, constructing for the marrow, first of all a complete covering of bone.

Bone was composed by him in the following manner. Having sifted pure and smooth earth he kneaded it and wetted it with marrow, and after that he put it into fire and then into water, and once more into fire and again into water — in this way by frequent transfers from one to the other he made it insoluble by either. Out of this he fashioned, as in a lathe, a globe made of bone, which he placed around the brain, and in this he left a narrow opening; and around the marrow of the neck and back he formed vertebrae which he placed under one another like pivots, beginning at the head and extending through the whole of the trunk. Thus wishing to preserve the entire seed, he enclosed it in a stone-like casing, inserting joints, and using in the formation of them the power of the other or diverse as an intermediate nature, that they might have motion and flexure. Then again, considering that the bone would be too brittle and inflexible, and when heated and again cooled would soon mortify and destroy the seed within — having this in view, he contrived the sinews and the flesh, that so binding all the members together by the sinews, which admitted of being stretched and relaxed about the vertebrae, he might thus make the body capable of flexion and extension, while the flesh would serve as a protection against the summer heat and against the winter cold, and also against falls, softly and easily yielding to external bodies, like articles made of felt; and containing in itself a warm moisture which in summer exudes and makes the surface damp, would impart a natural coolness to the whole body; and again in winter by the help of this internal warmth would form a very tolerable defence against the frost which surrounds it and attacks it from without. He who modelled us, considering these things, mixed earth with fire and water and blended them; and making a ferment of acid and salt, he mingled it with them and formed soft and succulent flesh. As for the sinews, he made them of a mixture of bone and unfermented flesh, attempered so as to be in a mean, and gave them a yellow colour; wherefore the sinews have a firmer and more glutinous nature than flesh, but a softer and moister nature than the bones. With these God covered the bones and marrow, binding them together by sinews, and then enshrouded them all in an upper covering of flesh. The more living and sensitive of the bones he enclosed in the thinnest film of flesh, and those which had the least life within them in the thickest and most solid flesh. So again on the joints of the bones, where reason indicated that no more was required, he placed only a thin covering of flesh, that it might not interfere with the flexion of our bodies and make them unwieldy because difficult to move; and also that it might not, by being crowded and pressed and matted together, destroy sensation by reason of its hardness, and impair the memory and dull the edge of intelligence. Wherefore also the thighs and the shanks and the hips, and the bones of the arms and the forearms, and other parts which have no joints, and the inner bones, which on account of the rarity of the soul in the marrow are destitute of reason — all these are abundantly provided with flesh; but such as have mind in them are in general less fleshy, except where the creator has made some part solely of flesh in order to give sensation — as, for example, the tongue. But commonly this is not the case. For the nature which comes into being and grows up in us by a law of necessity, does not admit of the combination of solid bone and much flesh with acute perceptions. More than any other part the framework of the head would have had them, if they could have co-existed, and the human race, having a strong and fleshy and sinewy head, would have had a life twice or many times as long as it now has, and also more healthy and free from pain. But our creators, considering whether they should make a longer-lived race which was worse, or a shorter-lived race which was better, came to the conclusion that every one ought to prefer a shorter span of life, which was better, to a longer one, which was worse; and therefore they covered the head with thin bone, but not with flesh and sinews, since it had no joints; and thus the head was added, having more wisdom and sensation than the rest of the body, but also being in every man far weaker. For these reasons and after this manner God placed the sinews at the extremity of the head, in a circle round the neck, and glued them together by the principle of likeness and fastened the extremities of the jawbones to them below the face, and the other sinews he dispersed throughout the body, fastening limb to limb. The framers of us framed the mouth, as now arranged, having teeth and tongue and lips, with a view to the necessary and the good contriving the way in for necessary purposes, the way out for the best purposes; for that is necessary which enters in and gives food to the body; but the river of speech, which flows out of a man and ministers to the intelligence, is the fairest and noblest of all streams. Still the head could neither be left a bare frame of bones, on account of the extremes of heat and cold in the different seasons, nor yet be allowed to be wholly covered, and so become dull and senseless by reason of an overgrowth of flesh. The fleshy nature was not therefore wholly dried up, but a large sort of peel was parted off and remained over, which is now called the skin. This met and grew by the help of the cerebral moisture, and became the circular envelopment of the head. And the moisture, rising up under the sutures, watered and closed in the skin upon the crown, forming a sort of knot. The diversity of the sutures was caused by the power of the courses of the soul and of the food, and the more these struggled against one another the more numerous they became, and fewer if the struggle were less violent. This skin the divine power pierced all round with fire, and out of the punctures which were thus made the moisture issued forth, and the liquid and heat which was pure came away, and a mixed part which was composed of the same material as the skin, and had a fineness equal to the punctures, was borne up by its own impulse and extended far outside the head, but being too slow to escape, was thrust back by the external air, and rolled up underneath the skin, where it took root. Thus the hair sprang up in the skin, being akin to it because it is like threads of leather, but rendered harder and closer through the pressure of the cold, by which each hair, while in process of separation from the skin, is compressed and cooled. Wherefore the creator formed the head hairy, making use of the causes which I have mentioned, and reflecting also that instead of flesh the brain needed the hair to be a light covering or guard, which would give shade in summer and shelter in winter, and at the same time would not impede our quickness of perception. From the combination of sinew, skin, and bone, in the structure of the finger, there arises a triple compound, which, when dried up, takes the form of one hard skin partaking of all three natures, and was fabricated by these second causes, but designed by mind which is the principal cause with an eye to the future. For our creators well knew that women and other animals would some day be framed out of men, and they further knew that many animals would require the use of nails for many purposes; wherefore they fashioned in men at their first creation the rudiments of nails. For this purpose and for these reasons they caused skin, hair, and nails to grow at the extremities of the limbs.

And now that all the parts and members of the mortal animal had come together, since its life of necessity consisted of fire and breath, and it therefore wasted away by dissolution and depletion, the gods contrived the following remedy: They mingled a nature akin to that of man with other forms and perceptions, and thus created another kind of animal. These are the trees and plants and seeds which have been improved by cultivation and are now domesticated among us; anciently there were only the wild kinds, which are older than the cultivated. For everything that partakes of life may be truly called a living being, and the animal of which we are now speaking partakes of the third kind of soul, which is said to be seated between the midriff and the navel, having no part in opinion or reason or mind, but only in feelings of pleasure and pain and the desires which accompany them. For this nature is always in a passive state, revolving in and about itself, repelling the motion from without and using its own, and accordingly is not endowed by nature with the power of observing or reflecting on its own concerns. Wherefore it lives and does not differ from a living being, but is fixed and rooted in the same spot, having no power of self-motion.

Now after the superior powers had created all these natures to be food for us who are of the inferior nature, they cut various channels through the body as through a garden, that it might be watered as from a running stream. In the first place, they cut two hidden channels or veins down the back where the skin and the flesh join, which answered severally to the right and left side of the body. These they let down along the backbone, so as to have the marrow of generation between them, where it was most likely to flourish, and in order that the stream coming down from above might flow freely to the other parts, and equalize the irrigation. In the next place, they divided the veins about the head, and interlacing them, they sent them in opposite directions; those coming from the right side they sent to the left of the body, and those from the left they diverted towards the right, so that they and the skin might together form a bond which should fasten the head to the body, since the crown of the head was not encircled by sinews; and also in order that the sensations from both sides might be distributed over the whole body. And next, they ordered the water-courses of the body in a manner which I will describe, and which will be more easily understood if we begin by admitting that all things which have lesser parts retain the greater, but the greater cannot retain the lesser. Now of all natures fire has the smallest parts, and therefore penetrates through earth and water and air and their compounds, nor can anything hold it. And a similar principle applies to the human belly; for when meats and drinks enter it, it holds them, but it cannot hold air and fire, because the particles of which they consist are smaller than its own structure.

These elements, therefore, God employed for the sake of distributing moisture from the belly into the veins, weaving together a network of fire and air like a weel, having at the entrance two lesser weels; further he constructed one of these with two openings, and from the lesser weels he extended cords reaching all round to the extremities of the network. All the interior of the net he made of fire, but the lesser weels and their cavity, of air. The network he took and spread over the newly-formed animal in the following manner:— He let the lesser weels pass into the mouth; there were two of them, and one he let down by the air-pipes into the lungs, the other by the side of the air-pipes into the belly. The former he divided into two branches, both of which he made to meet at the channels of the nose, so that when the way through the mouth did not act, the streams of the mouth as well were replenished through the nose. With the other cavity (i.e. of the greater weel) he enveloped the hollow parts of the body, and at one time he made all this to flow into the lesser weels, quite gently, for they are composed of air, and at another time he caused the lesser weels to flow back again; and the net he made to find a way in and out through the pores of the body, and the rays of fire which are bound fast within followed the passage of the air either way, never at any time ceasing so long as the mortal being holds together. This process, as we affirm, the name-giver named inspiration and expiration. And all this movement, active as well as passive, takes place in order that the body, being watered and cooled, may receive nourishment and life; for when the respiration is going in and out, and the fire, which is fast bound within, follows it, and ever and anon moving to and fro, enters through the belly and reaches the meat and drink, it dissolves them, and dividing them into small portions and guiding them through the passages where it goes, pumps them as from a fountain into the channels of the veins, and makes the stream of the veins flow through the body as through a conduit.

Let us once more consider the phenomena of respiration, and enquire into the causes which have made it what it is. They are as follows:— Seeing that there is no such thing as a vacuum into which any of those things which are moved can enter, and the breath is carried from us into the external air, the next point is, as will be clear to every one, that it does not go into a vacant space, but pushes its neighbour out of its place, and that which is thrust out in turn drives out its neighbour; and in this way everything of necessity at last comes round to that place from whence the breath came forth, and enters in there, and following the breath, fills up the vacant space; and this goes on like the rotation of a wheel, because there can be no such thing as a vacuum. Wherefore also the breast and the lungs, when they emit the breath, are replenished by the air which surrounds the body and which enters in through the pores of the flesh and is driven round in a circle; and again, the air which is sent away and passes out through the body forces the breath inwards through the passage of the mouth and the nostrils. Now the origin of this movement may be supposed to be as follows. In the interior of every animal the hottest part is that which is around the blood and veins; it is in a manner an internal fountain of fire, which we compare to the network of a creel, being woven all of fire and extended through the centre of the body, while the outer parts are composed of air. Now we must admit that heat naturally proceeds outward to its own place and to its kindred element; and as there are two exits for the heat, the one out through the body, and the other through the mouth and nostrils, when it moves towards the one, it drives round the air at the other, and that which is driven round falls into the fire and becomes warm, and that which goes forth is cooled. But when the heat changes its place, and the particles at the other exit grow warmer, the hotter air inclining in that direction and carried towards its native element, fire, pushes round the air at the other; and this being affected in the same way and communicating the same impulse, a circular motion swaying to and fro is produced by the double process, which we call inspiration and expiration.

The phenomena of medical cupping-glasses and of the swallowing of drink and of the projection of bodies, whether discharged in the air or bowled along the ground, are to be investigated on a similar principle; and swift and slow sounds, which appear to be high and low, and are sometimes discordant on account of their inequality, and then again harmonical on account of the equality of the motion which they excite in us. For when the motions of the antecedent swifter sounds begin to pause and the two are equalized, the slower sounds overtake the swifter and then propel them. When they overtake them they do not intrude a new and discordant motion, but introduce the beginnings of a slower, which answers to the swifter as it dies away, thus producing a single mixed expression out of high and low, whence arises a pleasure which even the unwise feel, and which to the wise becomes a higher sort of delight, being an imitation of divine harmony in mortal motions. Moreover, as to the flowing of water, the fall of the thunderbolt, and the marvels that are observed about the attraction of amber and the Heraclean stones — in none of these cases is there any attraction; but he who investigates rightly, will find that such wonderful phenomena are attributable to the combination of certain conditions — the non-existence of a vacuum, the fact that objects push one another round, and that they change places, passing severally into their proper positions as they are divided or combined.

Such as we have seen, is the nature and such are the causes of respiration, — the subject in which this discussion originated. For the fire cuts the food and following the breath surges up within, fire and breath rising together and filling the veins by drawing up out of the belly and pouring into them the cut portions of the food; and so the streams of food are kept flowing through the whole body in all animals. And fresh cuttings from kindred substances, whether the fruits of the earth or herb of the field, which God planted to be our daily food, acquire all sorts of colours by their inter-mixture; but red is the most pervading of them, being created by the cutting action of fire and by the impression which it makes on a moist substance; and hence the liquid which circulates in the body has a colour such as we have described. The liquid itself we call blood, which nourishes the flesh and the whole body, whence all parts are watered and empty places filled.

Now the process of repletion and evacuation is effected after the manner of the universal motion by which all kindred substances are drawn towards one another. For the external elements which surround us are always causing us to consume away, and distributing and sending off like to like; the particles of blood, too, which are divided and contained within the frame of the animal as in a sort of heaven, are compelled to imitate the motion of the universe. Each, therefore, of the divided parts within us, being carried to its kindred nature, replenishes the void. When more is taken away than flows in, then we decay, and when less, we grow and increase.

The frame of the entire creature when young has the triangles of each kind new, and may be compared to the keel of a vessel which is just off the stocks; they are locked firmly together and yet the whole mass is soft and delicate, being freshly formed of marrow and nurtured on milk. Now when the triangles out of which meats and drinks are composed come in from without, and are comprehended in the body, being older and weaker than the triangles already there, the frame of the body gets the better of them and its newer triangles cut them up, and so the animal grows great, being nourished by a multitude of similar particles. But when the roots of the triangles are loosened by having undergone many conflicts with many things in the course of time, they are no longer able to cut or assimilate the food which enters, but are themselves easily divided by the bodies which come in from without. In this way every animal is overcome and decays, and this affection is called old age. And at last, when the bonds by which the triangles of the marrow are united no longer hold, and are parted by the strain of existence, they in turn loosen the bonds of the soul, and she, obtaining a natural release, flies away with joy. For that which takes place according to nature is pleasant, but that which is contrary to nature is painful. And thus death, if caused by disease or produced by wounds, is painful and violent; but that sort of death which comes with old age and fulfils the debt of nature is the easiest of deaths, and is accompanied with pleasure rather than with pain.

Now every one can see whence diseases arise. There are four natures out of which the body is compacted, earth and fire and water and air, and the unnatural excess or defect of these, or the change of any of them from its own natural place into another, or — since there are more kinds than one of fire and of the other elements — the assumption by any of these of a wrong kind, or any similar irregularity, produces disorders and diseases; for when any of them is produced or changed in a manner contrary to nature, the parts which were previously cool grow warm, and those which were dry become moist, and the light become heavy, and the heavy light; all sorts of changes occur. For, as we affirm, a thing can only remain the same with itself, whole and sound, when the same is added to it, or subtracted from it, in the same respect and in the same manner and in due proportion; and whatever comes or goes away in violation of these laws causes all manner of changes and infinite diseases and corruptions. Now there is a second class of structures which are also natural, and this affords a second opportunity of observing diseases to him who would understand them. For whereas marrow and bone and flesh and sinews are composed of the four elements, and the blood, though after another manner, is likewise formed out of them, most diseases originate in the way which I have described; but the worst of all owe their severity to the fact that the generation of these substances proceeds in a wrong order; they are then destroyed. For the natural order is that the flesh and sinews should be made of blood, the sinews out of the fibres to which they are akin, and the flesh out of the clots which are formed when the fibres are separated. And the glutinous and rich matter which comes away from the sinews and the flesh, not only glues the flesh to the bones, but nourishes and imparts growth to the bone which surrounds the marrow; and by reason of the solidity of the bones, that which filters through consists of the purest and smoothest and oiliest sort of triangles, dropping like dew from the bones and watering the marrow. Now when each process takes place in this order, health commonly results; when in the opposite order, disease. For when the flesh becomes decomposed and sends back the wasting substance into the veins, then an over-supply of blood of diverse kinds, mingling with air in the veins, having variegated colours and bitter properties, as well as acid and saline qualities, contains all sorts of bile and serum and phlegm. For all things go the wrong way, and having become corrupted, first they taint the blood itself, and then ceasing to give nourishment to the body they are carried along the veins in all directions, no longer preserving the order of their natural courses, but at war with themselves, because they receive no good from one another, and are hostile to the abiding constitution of the body, which they corrupt and dissolve. The oldest part of the flesh which is corrupted, being hard to decompose, from long burning grows black, and from being everywhere corroded becomes bitter, and is injurious to every part of the body which is still uncorrupted. Sometimes, when the bitter element is refined away, the black part assumes an acidity which takes the place of the bitterness; at other times the bitterness being tinged with blood has a redder colour; and this, when mixed with black, takes the hue of grass; and again, an auburn colour mingles with the bitter matter when new flesh is decomposed by the fire which surrounds the internal flame; — to all which symptoms some physician perhaps, or rather some philosopher, who had the power of seeing in many dissimilar things one nature deserving of a name, has assigned the common name of bile. But the other kinds of bile are variously distinguished by their colours. As for serum, that sort which is the watery part of blood is innocent, but that which is a secretion of black and acid bile is malignant when mingled by the power of heat with any salt substance, and is then called acid phlegm. Again, the substance which is formed by the liquefaction of new and tender flesh when air is present, if inflated and encased in liquid so as to form bubbles, which separately are invisible owing to their small size, but when collected are of a bulk which is visible, and have a white colour arising out of the generation of foam — all this decomposition of tender flesh when intermingled with air is termed by us white phlegm. And the whey or sediment of newly-formed phlegm is sweat and tears, and includes the various daily discharges by which the body is purified. Now all these become causes of disease when the blood is not replenished in a natural manner by food and drink but gains bulk from opposite sources in violation of the laws of nature. When the several parts of the flesh are separated by disease, if the foundation remains, the power of the disorder is only half as great, and there is still a prospect of an easy recovery; but when that which binds the flesh to the bones is diseased, and no longer being separated from the muscles and sinews, ceases to give nourishment to the bone and to unite flesh and bone, and from being oily and smooth and glutinous becomes rough and salt and dry, owing to bad regimen, then all the substance thus corrupted crumbles away under the flesh and the sinews, and separates from the bone, and the fleshy parts fall away from their foundation and leave the sinews bare and full of brine, and the flesh again gets into the circulation of the blood and makes the previously-mentioned disorders still greater. And if these bodily affections be severe, still worse are the prior disorders; as when the bone itself, by reason of the density of the flesh, does not obtain sufficient air, but becomes mouldy and hot and gangrened and receives no nutriment, and the natural process is inverted, and the bone crumbling passes into the food, and the food into the flesh, and the flesh again falling into the blood makes all maladies that may occur more virulent than those already mentioned. But the worst case of all is when the marrow is diseased, either from excess or defect; and this is the cause of the very greatest and most fatal disorders, in which the whole course of the body is reversed.

There is a third class of diseases which may be conceived of as arising in three ways; for they are produced sometimes by wind, and sometimes by phlegm, and sometimes by bile. When the lung, which is the dispenser of the air to the body, is obstructed by rheums and its passages are not free, some of them not acting, while through others too much air enters, then the parts which are unrefreshed by air corrode, while in other parts the excess of air forcing its way through the veins distorts them and decomposing the body is enclosed in the midst of it and occupies the midriff; thus numberless painful diseases are produced, accompanied by copious sweats. And oftentimes when the flesh is dissolved in the body, wind, generated within and unable to escape, is the source of quite as much pain as the air coming in from without; but the greatest pain is felt when the wind gets about the sinews and the veins of the shoulders, and swells them up, and so twists back the great tendons and the sinews which are connected with them.

These disorders are called tetanus and opisthotonus, by reason of the tension which accompanies them. The cure of them is difficult; relief is in most cases given by fever supervening. The white phlegm, though dangerous when detained within by reason of the air-bubbles, yet if it can communicate with the outside air, is less severe, and only discolours the body, generating leprous eruptions and similar diseases. When it is mingled with black bile and dispersed about the courses of the head, which are the divinest part of us, the attack if coming on in sleep, is not so severe; but when assailing those who are awake it is hard to be got rid of, and being an affection of a sacred part, is most justly called sacred. An acid and salt phlegm, again, is the source of all those diseases which take the form of catarrh, but they have many names because the places into which they flow are manifold.

Inflammations of the body come from burnings and inflamings, and all of them originate in bile. When bile finds a means of discharge, it boils up and sends forth all sorts of tumours; but when imprisoned within, it generates many inflammatory diseases, above all when mingled with pure blood; since it then displaces the fibres which are scattered about in the blood and are designed to maintain the balance of rare and dense, in order that the blood may not be so liquefied by heat as to exude from the pores of the body, nor again become too dense and thus find a difficulty in circulating through the veins. The fibres are so constituted as to maintain this balance; and if any one brings them all together when the blood is dead and in process of cooling, then the blood which remains becomes fluid, but if they are left alone, they soon congeal by reason of the surrounding cold. The fibres having this power over the blood, bile, which is only stale blood, and which from being flesh is dissolved again into blood, at the first influx coming in little by little, hot and liquid, is congealed by the power of the fibres; and so congealing and made to cool, it produces internal cold and shuddering. When it enters with more of a flood and overcomes the fibres by its heat, and boiling up throws them into disorder, if it have power enough to maintain its supremacy, it penetrates the marrow and burns up what may be termed the cables of the soul, and sets her free; but when there is not so much of it, and the body though wasted still holds out, the bile is itself mastered, and is either utterly banished, or is thrust through the veins into the lower or upper belly, and is driven out of the body like an exile from a state in which there has been civil war; whence arise diarrhoeas and dysenteries, and all such disorders. When the constitution is disordered by excess of fire, continuous heat and fever are the result; when excess of air is the cause, then the fever is quotidian; when of water, which is a more sluggish element than either fire or air, then the fever is a tertian; when of earth, which is the most sluggish of the four, and is only purged away in a four-fold period, the result is a quartan fever, which can with difficulty be shaken off.

Such is the manner in which diseases of the body arise; the disorders of the soul, which depend upon the body, originate as follows. We must acknowledge disease of the mind to be a want of intelligence; and of this there are two kinds; to wit, madness and ignorance. In whatever state a man experiences either of them, that state may be called disease; and excessive pains and pleasures are justly to be regarded as the greatest diseases to which the soul is liable. For a man who is in great joy or in great pain, in his unreasonable eagerness to attain the one and to avoid the other, is not able to see or to hear anything rightly; but he is mad, and is at the time utterly incapable of any participation in reason. He who has the seed about the spinal marrow too plentiful and overflowing, like a tree overladen with fruit, has many throes, and also obtains many pleasures in his desires and their offspring, and is for the most part of his life deranged, because his pleasures and pains are so very great; his soul is rendered foolish and disordered by his body; yet he is regarded not as one diseased, but as one who is voluntarily bad, which is a mistake. The truth is that the intemperance of love is a disease of the soul due chiefly to the moisture and fluidity which is produced in one of the elements by the loose consistency of the bones. And in general, all that which is termed the incontinence of pleasure and is deemed a reproach under the idea that the wicked voluntarily do wrong is not justly a matter for reproach. For no man is voluntarily bad; but the bad become bad by reason of an ill disposition of the body and bad education, things which are hateful to every man and happen to him against his will. And in the case of pain too in like manner the soul suffers much evil from the body. For where the acid and briny phlegm and other bitter and bilious humours wander about in the body, and find no exit or escape, but are pent up within and mingle their own vapours with the motions of the soul, and are blended with them, they produce all sorts of diseases, more or fewer, and in every degree of intensity; and being carried to the three places of the soul, whichever they may severally assail, they create infinite varieties of ill-temper and melancholy, of rashness and cowardice, and also of forgetfulness and stupidity. Further, when to this evil constitution of body evil forms of government are added and evil discourses are uttered in private as well as in public, and no sort of instruction is given in youth to cure these evils, then all of us who are bad become bad from two causes which are entirely beyond our control. In such cases the planters are to blame rather than the plants, the educators rather than the educated. But however that may be, we should endeavour as far as we can by education, and studies, and learning, to avoid vice and attain virtue; this, however, is part of another subject.

There is a corresponding enquiry concerning the mode of treatment by which the mind and the body are to be preserved, about which it is meet and right that I should say a word in turn; for it is more our duty to speak of the good than of the evil. Everything that is good is fair, and the fair is not without proportion, and the animal which is to be fair must have due proportion. Now we perceive lesser symmetries or proportions and reason about them, but of the highest and greatest we take no heed; for there is no proportion or disproportion more productive of health and disease, and virtue and vice, than that between soul and body. This however we do not perceive, nor do we reflect that when a weak or small frame is the vehicle of a great and mighty soul, or conversely, when a little soul is encased in a large body, then the whole animal is not fair, for it lacks the most important of all symmetries; but the due proportion of mind and body is the fairest and loveliest of all sights to him who has the seeing eye. Just as a body which has a leg too long, or which is unsymmetrical in some other respect, is an unpleasant sight, and also, when doing its share of work, is much distressed and makes convulsive efforts, and often stumbles through awkwardness, and is the cause of infinite evil to its own self — in like manner we should conceive of the double nature which we call the living being; and when in this compound there is an impassioned soul more powerful than the body, that soul, I say, convulses and fills with disorders the whole inner nature of man; and when eager in the pursuit of some sort of learning or study, causes wasting; or again, when teaching or disputing in private or in public, and strifes and controversies arise, inflames and dissolves the composite frame of man and introduces rheums; and the nature of this phenomenon is not understood by most professors of medicine, who ascribe it to the opposite of the real cause. And once more, when a body large and too strong for the soul is united to a small and weak intelligence, then inasmuch as there are two desires natural to man — one of food for the sake of the body, and one of wisdom for the sake of the diviner part of us — then, I say, the motions of the stronger, getting the better and increasing their own power, but making the soul dull, and stupid, and forgetful, engender ignorance, which is the greatest of diseases. There is one protection against both kinds of disproportion:— that we should not move the body without the soul or the soul without the body, and thus they will be on their guard against each other, and be healthy and well balanced. And therefore the mathematician or any one else whose thoughts are much absorbed in some intellectual pursuit, must allow his body also to have due exercise, and practise gymnastic; and he who is careful to fashion the body, should in turn impart to the soul its proper motions, and should cultivate music and all philosophy, if he would deserve to be called truly fair and truly good. And the separate parts should be treated in the same manner, in imitation of the pattern of the universe; for as the body is heated and also cooled within by the elements which enter into it, and is again dried up and moistened by external things, and experiences these and the like affections from both kinds of motions, the result is that the body if given up to motion when in a state of quiescence is overmastered and perishes; but if any one, in imitation of that which we call the foster-mother and nurse of the universe, will not allow the body ever to be inactive, but is always producing motions and agitations through its whole extent, which form the natural defence against other motions both internal and external, and by moderate exercise reduces to order according to their affinities the particles and affections which are wandering about the body, as we have already said when speaking of the universe, he will not allow enemy placed by the side of enemy to stir up wars and disorders in the body, but he will place friend by the side of friend, so as to create health. Now of all motions that is the best which is produced in a thing by itself, for it is most akin to the motion of thought and of the universe; but that motion which is caused by others is not so good, and worst of all is that which moves the body, when at rest, in parts only and by some external agency. Wherefore of all modes of purifying and re- uniting the body the best is gymnastic; the next best is a surging motion, as in sailing or any other mode of conveyance which is not fatiguing; the third sort of motion may be of use in a case of extreme necessity, but in any other will be adopted by no man of sense: I mean the purgative treatment of physicians; for diseases unless they are very dangerous should not be irritated by medicines, since every form of disease is in a manner akin to the living being, whose complex frame has an appointed term of life. For not the whole race only, but each individual — barring inevitable accidents — comes into the world having a fixed span, and the triangles in us are originally framed with power to last for a certain time, beyond which no man can prolong his life. And this holds also of the constitution of diseases; if any one regardless of the appointed time tries to subdue them by medicine, he only aggravates and multiplies them. Wherefore we ought always to manage them by regimen, as far as a man can spare the time, and not provoke a disagreeable enemy by medicines.

Enough of the composite animal, and of the body which is a part of him, and of the manner in which a man may train and be trained by himself so as to live most according to reason: and we must above and before all provide that the element which is to train him shall be the fairest and best adapted to that purpose. A minute discussion of this subject would be a serious task; but if, as before, I am to give only an outline, the subject may not unfitly be summed up as follows.

I have often remarked that there are three kinds of soul located within us, having each of them motions, and I must now repeat in the fewest words possible, that one part, if remaining inactive and ceasing from its natural motion, must necessarily become very weak, but that which is trained and exercised, very strong. Wherefore we should take care that the movements of the different parts of the soul should be in due proportion.

And we should consider that God gave the sovereign part of the human soul to be the divinity of each one, being that part which, as we say, dwells at the top of the body, and inasmuch as we are a plant not of an earthly but of a heavenly growth, raises us from earth to our kindred who are in heaven. And in this we say truly; for the divine power suspended the head and root of us from that place where the generation of the soul first began, and thus made the whole body upright. When a man is always occupied with the cravings of desire and ambition, and is eagerly striving to satisfy them, all his thoughts must be mortal, and, as far as it is possible altogether to become such, he must be mortal every whit, because he has cherished his mortal part. But he who has been earnest in the love of knowledge and of true wisdom, and has exercised his intellect more than any other part of him, must have thoughts immortal and divine, if he attain truth, and in so far as human nature is capable of sharing in immortality, he must altogether be immortal; and since he is ever cherishing the divine power, and has the divinity within him in perfect order, he will be perfectly happy. Now there is only one way of taking care of things, and this is to give to each the food and motion which are natural to it. And the motions which are naturally akin to the divine principle within us are the thoughts and revolutions of the universe. These each man should follow, and correct the courses of the head which were corrupted at our birth, and by learning the harmonies and revolutions of the universe, should assimilate the thinking being to the thought, renewing his original nature, and having assimilated them should attain to that perfect life which the gods have set before mankind, both for the present and the future.

Thus our original design of discoursing about the universe down to the creation of man is nearly completed. A brief mention may be made of the generation of other animals, so far as the subject admits of brevity; in this manner our argument will best attain a due proportion. On the subject of animals, then, the following remarks may be offered. Of the men who came into the world, those who were cowards or led unrighteous lives may with reason be supposed to have changed into the nature of women in the second generation. And this was the reason why at that time the gods created in us the desire of sexual intercourse, contriving in man one animated substance, and in woman another, which they formed respectively in the following manner. The outlet for drink by which liquids pass through the lung under the kidneys and into the bladder, which receives and then by the pressure of the air emits them, was so fashioned by them as to penetrate also into the body of the marrow, which passes from the head along the neck and through the back, and which in the preceding discourse we have named the seed. And the seed having life, and becoming endowed with respiration, produces in that part in which it respires a lively desire of emission, and thus creates in us the love of procreation. Wherefore also in men the organ of generation becoming rebellious and masterful, like an animal disobedient to reason, and maddened with the sting of lust, seeks to gain absolute sway; and the same is the case with the so-called womb or matrix of women; the animal within them is desirous of procreating children, and when remaining unfruitful long beyond its proper time, gets discontented and angry, and wandering in every direction through the body, closes up the passages of the breath, and, by obstructing respiration, drives them to extremity, causing all varieties of disease, until at length the desire and love of the man and the woman, bringing them together and as it were plucking the fruit from the tree, sow in the womb, as in a field, animals unseen by reason of their smallness and without form; these again are separated and matured within; they are then finally brought out into the light, and thus the generation of animals is completed.

Thus were created women and the female sex in general. But the race of birds was created out of innocent light-minded men, who, although their minds were directed toward heaven, imagined, in their simplicity, that the clearest demonstration of the things above was to be obtained by sight; these were remodelled and transformed into birds, and they grew feathers instead of hair. The race of wild pedestrian animals, again, came from those who had no philosophy in any of their thoughts, and never considered at all about the nature of the heavens, because they had ceased to use the courses of the head, but followed the guidance of those parts of the soul which are in the breast. In consequence of these habits of theirs they had their front-legs and their heads resting upon the earth to which they were drawn by natural affinity; and the crowns of their heads were elongated and of all sorts of shapes, into which the courses of the soul were crushed by reason of disuse. And this was the reason why they were created quadrupeds and polypods: God gave the more senseless of them the more support that they might be more attracted to the earth. And the most foolish of them, who trail their bodies entirely upon the ground and have no longer any need of feet, he made without feet to crawl upon the earth. The fourth class were the inhabitants of the water: these were made out of the most entirely senseless and ignorant of all, whom the transformers did not think any longer worthy of pure respiration, because they possessed a soul which was made impure by all sorts of transgression; and instead of the subtle and pure medium of air, they gave them the deep and muddy sea to be their element of respiration; and hence arose the race of fishes and oysters, and other aquatic animals, which have received the most remote habitations as a punishment of their outlandish ignorance. These are the laws by which animals pass into one another, now, as ever, changing as they lose or gain wisdom and folly.

We may now say that our discourse about the nature of the universe has an end. The world has received animals, mortal and immortal, and is fulfilled with them, and has become a visible animal containing the visible — the sensible God who is the image of the intellectual, the greatest, best, fairest, most perfect — the one only-begotten heaven.

CPSIA information can be obtained
at www.ICGtesting.com
Printed in the USA
LVHW062219050822
725273LV00017B/944